Walk like Jesus Walked

Volume 1

Learning

to

Walk

Loren VanGalder

Spiritual Father Publications

ISBN-13: 978-1-7336556-1-3

Contents

Introduction

An invitation: "Would you like to walk as Jesus walked?"

The theme of this book is 1 John 2:5–6:

> By this we may be sure that we are in [Christ]:
>
> whoever says, 'I abide in him',
>
> ought to walk just as he walked.

God's Word translation says: *Those who say that they live in him must live the same way he lived.*

This is a test, a way to be sure that you are in Christ, or (from other translations), *united* to him or *living* in him. Are you really saved? Do you ever have doubts? Are you OK with God?

Talk is cheap. It is possible to say a prayer for salvation and go to church regularly without living in Christ or being united to him. Sadly, many people's faith is mere talk, but, like James 2:20 says, *faith without works is dead.* You can say you are a Christian and everything is fine between you and God. You can say that you are abiding in Christ, but how is your daily walk?

The test of a living faith is walking as Jesus walked

Wow! Is that even possible?

Yes! If it weren't, it wouldn't be in the Bible!

It is possible to walk as Jesus walked! That in itself is amazing!

It is God's will for your life!

He will help you do it!

A few years ago, it was fashionable to wear a wristband with the initials WWJD (What Would Jesus Do?). They were onto something; too bad more of them didn't actually do what Jesus did.

This is the first of four volumes, covering the basics of Christian discipleship. Unlike most similar books, this one is based on Jesus' example and teachings. The idea is to experience what it was like to walk with Jesus while he was on this earth. The second book goes deeper into how to live in the Kingdom of God (drawing heavily on the Sermon on the Mount), the third studies Jesus' life as an exemplary leader, and the last book is a study of Acts, and how the Holy Spirit empowered the early church to walk like Jesus.

The world is spiritually hungry, but is tired of our hypocrisy and lack of love and power. More than ever, we need healing and deliverance, but there are few real miracles. And the answer is so simple! It's Jesus! What do you think? Jesus invites you to walk as he walked. Do you want to? He is your example to study and imitate.

To this you were called, because Christ suffered for you, leaving you an example, that you should follow in his steps.

(1 Peter 2:21)

1

Getting Started

Before you can walk, there's a decision you have to make: you need a living relationship with Jesus. The entrance is here, in Matthew 7:13-14:

"Enter through the narrow gate. For wide is the gate and broad is the road that leads to destruction, and many enter through it. But small is the gate and narrow the road that leads to life, and only a few find it.

Lights, attractions, TV, and internet all beckon us to the wide gate; we naturally end up on the broad road. You have to work and look hard to find the narrow road; only a few faithful soldiers of Christ are pointing people to the small gate. Are you among the few that have made it through? Do you find yourself on a rough road? Did someone tell you it would be easy? Have you considered getting back on the broad, easy road?

Most of the crowd following Jesus was still on the broad road to destruction; possibly the majority of "believers" in the stadiums and mega-churches are on that road. Thousands followed Jesus when the wine was flowing, the bread was multiplying, and the blind were seeing, but only 120 were left after his crucifixion. Jesus even lost one of the Twelve, and almost lost Peter! It's not easy being a Christian and walking with Jesus! Are you sure you want to? Think about it. Do you really believe that the alternative is an eternity in hell?

Do you want to be Jesus' disciple?

A disciple is a student, sitting at the feet of his master, learning from him, and following his teaching. In Luke 14, Jesus shared five requirements for discipleship.

[25] Large crowds were traveling with Jesus, and turning to them he said: [26] "If anyone comes to me and does not hate father and mother, wife and children, brothers and sisters—yes, even their own life—such a person cannot be my disciple.

1. Hate your family

You have to hate the people you love most! But didn't Jesus say we were to *love,* even our enemies? Of course. It's always dangerous to pick out a few words from any teacher; you have to analyze their entire teaching. Jesus is purposely saying something extreme to wake the crowd up and get their attention; he's making it clear that he must always be our priority!

Jesus' own family didn't understand his mission. It is common for a family to reject the "fanatic." In the past, a Catholic family might disown someone who became Pentecostal. That still happens in some places, and Muslims routinely pay with their lives if they get baptized. There will likely be situations where we have to choose between our family and Jesus; we must choose Jesus.

2. Hate your own life

This doesn't mean you can't be Jesus' disciple if you are grateful for the good life God has blessed you with. But if you love your life too much, you will do everything possible to save it—even if it means renouncing Christ. Many believers in the early church lost their lives because they were disciples of Christ; today, there are more martyrs than ever before. The natural instinct is to protect your life. Jesus said we must lay down our lives for others. Some have had such a rough life that they genuinely hate it. They are great candidates for discipleship!

27And whoever does not carry their cross and follow me cannot be my disciple.

3. Carry your cross

At that point, the disciples had no idea that Jesus would die on a cross, but Jesus says everyone has a cross! You must crucify your flesh and your desires, and deny yourself.

What is your cross? It may be heavy. It could be a person, a weakness, a sickness, or some other burden.

4. Follow Jesus

Jesus leads, you follow. He goes first. If you follow in his footsteps, you will end up walking as he walked.

We will see the last requirement for discipleship in verse 33, but first, he provides two examples to help us understand what he has just said.

28 "Suppose one of you wants to build a tower. Won't you first sit down and estimate the cost to see if you have enough money to complete it? 29 For if you lay the foundation and are not able to finish it, everyone who sees it will ridicule you, 30 saying, 'This person began to build and wasn't able to finish.'

Finish what you start

It's wonderful to go through that small door, invite Jesus into your life, and start walking the narrow road with him, especially in the emotion of an anointed worship service, with friends and family surrounding you. But it's more important to make it to the end. The hard part is walking the walk day after day, at home and on the job. Unfortunately, we often fail to share the cost of discipleship with a new believer. It's crucial to be aware of all that is involved in being a Christian, and to count the cost. That is not only true for your relationship with Jesus, but for any project you undertake for the Lord—and for all of life.

The church is full of projects that good people started with a lot of faith; men who began building a church or other ministry but never finished it. Most of us have some project that we started, but then got tired or never had the time or resources to finish it. And we leave it sitting there. Sometimes we put it out of sight, an annoying reminder of our poor planning, or our spouses may constantly point out the need to finish it. It's not that hard to start a project; there are many visionaries, but they need to connect with engineers and detail-oriented individuals who can make it a reality.

When you start a project, see it through to completion. Think about how to complete it before you begin. I know faith is important; God may call us to take a step of faith without knowing where the money will come from to accomplish it. Some say it shows a lack of faith to make plans; we must simply be guided by the Spirit. However, Jesus says that before acting, the wise man sits down, prays, plans, and calculates the cost. It is important to Jesus that no one makes fun of his followers because they fail to finish what they started. That is not honoring to him.

In this context, Jesus is primarily talking about clearly understanding what it means to go through the narrow gate. It is dangerous to make that decision under pressure, too quickly, and based only on emotions. It is the most important decision of your life. For real! Think it through carefully. How will it impact your family and your lifestyle?

Consider the cost of the battle

[31] *"Or suppose a king is about to go to war against another king. Won't he first sit down and consider whether he is able with ten thousand men to oppose the one coming against him with twenty thousand?* [32] *If he is not able, he will send a delegation while the other is still a long way off and will ask for terms of peace.*

Entering the small gate won't get you out of the line of fire. The devil still attacks and tempts believers on the narrow road. In fact, you are *"about to go to war"* when you decide to be Christ's disciple. The battle is not as fierce on the broad road, because you are already in the devil's camp.

Even though we may be few in number, God enables us to confront demonic principalities and powers, and all the things of this world. But we need to study the enemy and choose our battles, guided by the Lord. He may send us into a battle vastly outnumbered, but he has also given us intelligence, and will give us wisdom.

Be realistic about your battles. Open your eyes and figure out who your real enemies are. Obviously, we're not going to make peace with the devil, but you may need to acknowledge that there are battles at work, at home, or in the community that you can't win. Sometimes, we need to give up the battle, humble ourselves, and find an alternative solution to the problem.

The "other king" that you have to face may be God himself. You have been the king of your life, but now you have discovered someone stronger than you. You may have already spent years fighting God. It's a battle you will never win. You can keep fighting—and lose your life for eternity. Or you can make peace with God, give your life to him, surrender, and become his disciple.

There is also a valuable lesson here about spiritual warfare. I have seen men come into a city that is the devil's stronghold. They talk very confidently about how they are going to win that city for Christ and destroy the enemy, but they haven't counted the personal cost of the battle. They haven't considered that their church is small and isn't used to fasting and spiritual warfare. They haven't taken into account the divisions among churches in that community. Months later, they sneak out of town with their faith and families in ruins.

In these two examples, in their context, Jesus is impressing on us the cost of discipleship. Be careful of how you present the Gospel. Of course, we talk about blessings like forgiveness of sins, eternal life, and the power of the Holy Spirit. But also tell them how much they have to give up. It's not easy to carry a cross every day. Have you counted the cost of following Jesus?

Jesus finished this message with the fifth cost of discipleship. Perhaps he saved this for last and presented these two examples first because he knew that this last one would be the most challenging.

[33] In the same way, those of you who do not give up everything you have cannot be my disciples.

5. Give up everything you own

It is hard for a rich man to be Christ's disciple; he has too much to give up. It is easier for a poor man who has very little, or a prisoner who has already lost everything.

What does it mean to give up everything you possess? Sometimes Jesus would tell a rich man to sell everything and give it to the poor, but it may simply be a matter of changing one's perspective. Your possessions are no longer yours; you have to lay them down at the feet of Jesus. Give everything to him. And if he says you need to give that car to someone who needs it, you have to obey him. Life is no longer about what we own; it's about what we are. It's not about material things. We must let them go. Many people are unable to take this step. It is probably the most concrete part of discipleship, which affects every aspect of your life. We can spiritualize carrying our cross and rationalize our love for our family, but Jesus is clear that it is *"everything you have."* Jesus had nothing. It's liberating to give up all your "stuff!" If we are going to walk as Jesus walked, we can't be wrapped up in the material things of this world. How many Christians do you know who have given up everything they have? It reminds me of what Paul said in 1 Corinthians 7:29–31:

What I mean, brothers and sisters, is that the time is short. From now on those who have wives should live as if they do not; those who mourn, as if they did not; those who are happy, as if they were not; those who buy something, as if it were not theirs to keep; those who use the things of the world, as if not engrossed in them. For this world in its present form is passing away.

It's not sinful to enjoy the things of the world, just as it's not sinful to have a wife. It is a matter of where your heart is at. In this entire passage, Christ has spoken in extremes (hating your family and your own life), and, as always, it must be balanced with other Scriptures. As Jesus said in Matthew 6:32–33, after speaking about the basic material goods of this life:

For the pagans run after all these things, and your heavenly Father knows that you need them. But seek first his kingdom and his righteousness, and all these things will be given to you as well.

In this first chapter, we have looked at some of the toughest verses in the Gospels! If you want to be Jesus' disciple, he requires everything. It can't be Christ and your spouse, or Christ and your work, or Christ and your sports. Jesus has to be everything. Number one. Priority. Jesus knew that few would accept these requirements. Few would walk as he walked. But that's okay. Consider how one solitary life changed the world. God doesn't need a lot of people. A church of fifteen people walking as Jesus walked is much more powerful than a church of one thousand walking the broad road, caught up in their possessions and all the things of this world.

Are you ready to take these steps and walk as Jesus walked?

2

To Walk, You Must be Born (Again)

John 3

D on't get discouraged! Yes, being Jesus' disciple and walking as he walked can seem overwhelming. Israel's experience throughout the Old Testament makes obeying God seem impossible, and it *is* impossible in our flesh. But Jesus has a fantastic offer: You can be born again and start all over, learning to walk in his power.

¹Now there was a Pharisee, a man named Nicodemus who was a member of the Jewish ruling council.

Jesus was a phenomenon when he walked this earth, attracting huge crowds. He fed 5,000, mostly ordinary people, with five loaves of bread and two fish. He wasn't popular with the Jewish leaders, and for good reason: they feared the Romans, and didn't want to jeopardize the little independence they enjoyed.

Who was Nicodemus?

Nicodemus was a member of the Sanhedrin (the governing council that sought to kill Jesus), and a Pharisee (the most religious group of that day). The Pharisees were Jesus' fiercest critics, in large part because they claimed he didn't keep the law.

What he didn't honor were all the additions made to God's Word through the years, but he perfectly kept the God-given law.

Nicodemus had heard about Jesus, but doesn't strike us as a man who would seek Jesus out or believe in him. He had money and position, but he wanted something more. He had to find out what drew so many people to Jesus. To overcome all the obstacles and seek him out, Nicodemus must have felt a sense of urgency.

What have you heard about Jesus? Do you really know him? Nicodemus was seeking Jesus. You are reading this book because you want to be closer to Jesus. Nicodemus' life is about to change. If you still don't have a living relationship with Jesus, your life can also change.

An undercover visit

² He came to Jesus at night and said, "Rabbi, we know that you are a teacher who has come from God. For no one could perform the signs you are doing if God were not with him."

First, Nicodemus had to talk to someone who knew where to find Jesus at night. Christ had no home, office, or synagogue; he was always on the move and changing where he stayed, and was usually surrounded by a crowd (or at least the twelve disciples). Nicodemus had to see Jesus in private. If the Sanhedrin learned that he had gone to speak with Jesus, he could lose his position. He may have disguised himself as a peasant or fisherman and gone late at night.

Here was a man who had studied Jesus and called him "Rabbi" (a title of respect that means "teacher"). He had listened to Jesus' teaching and was impressed with his authority. He says, "*We know*" that you have come from God; maybe other Pharisees also believed that, but didn't want it made public (some said that Jesus came from Satan). He was also impressed with the signs

Jesus performed, which confirmed to Nicodemus that God must be with him.

Miracles were an important confirmation of God's power in Jesus' life, although we know that the devil can also do signs to deceive people, like the plagues in Egypt. These two things—the word, and signs and miracles to confirm it—were always part of Jesus' ministry, and, later, the disciples' ministry. They should be part of our ministry today; there should be some evidence, some sign, that our teaching is the truth.

A theological discussion

"Rabbi, we know that you are a teacher who has come from God. For no one could perform the signs you are doing if God were not with him." Nicodemus didn't question Jesus; he simply declared the little he knew about him. So far, it was a theological discussion, similar to the religious arguments many people engage in today:

- Why are there so many hypocrites in the church?
- What about all the contradictions in the Bible?
- Why does God allow suffering?
- Did Cain marry his sister?

It can be a good head trip, but it has nothing to do with your life. Jesus didn't respond to what he said, but changed the topic and immediately went deeper (Jesus loved doing that!):

³ Jesus replied, "Very truly I tell you, no one can see the kingdom of God unless they are born again."

How to see the kingdom of God

Nicodemus probably thought he was already in the kingdom: He was a Jew (part of God's chosen people), living in Jerusalem (the holy city), and a highly educated Pharisee. Today, many people believe they are in the kingdom because they were baptized as babies, come from a Christian family, or attend church.

Do you want to see the kingdom? What is the kingdom of God? It's not a place; Jesus said the kingdom is within us (Luke 17:21), but in the Lord's Prayer, we say, 'May your kingdom come.' There is a coming kingdom, when God will establish his reign here on earth. God's kingdom is present wherever he is honored and obeyed as King; where he is in charge. We want to extend his kingdom, knowing that it offers the best life possible on this earth. Many of us occupy the throne of our lives; we do things our way. To enter the kingdom, you must give your life, family, money, dreams, and future to Jesus, trusting that he knows better than you how to live. You can put Jesus on the throne of your life right now, and enter his kingdom.

Nicodemus wasn't thinking on a spiritual level; he hadn't come to the point of leaving everything to seek God and enter his kingdom.

How can you be born again?

4 "How can someone be born when they are old?" Nicodemus asked. "Surely they cannot enter a second time into their mother's womb to be born!"

Nicodemus wasn't stupid; he knew that what Jesus said was impossible. When we try to understand the Bible or a relationship to God logically, it looks impossible:

- Science tells us that no one can walk on water.
- A man dead for four days cannot come back to life.
- You can't feed thousands of people with a few loaves of bread and a couple of fish.

God wants to change your way of thinking and your way of seeing things. We must see life through the eyes of faith, with God's eyes. Jesus is talking about a supernatural life. Are you tired of life in the flesh, limited by the laws of nature? God offers you a life where everything is possible.

It is true that no one can return to their mother's womb, but that doesn't mean that you can't be born again in another dimension.

5 Jesus answered, "Very truly I tell you, no one can enter the kingdom of God unless they are born of water and the Spirit.6 Flesh gives birth to flesh, but the Spirit gives birth to spirit. 7 You should not be surprised at my saying, 'You must be born again.'

We all are born of the flesh. You don't have the choice to say: "No, I don't want to be part of that family, in that country, with so much suffering." You are the result of the love between your father and mother (hopefully, because, sadly, sometimes that is not the case). Now you can decide to be born spiritually; not making that decision is to decide that you don't want to enter the kingdom. There is a saying: born once, die twice; born twice, die once. We are all going to die in the flesh, but you don't have to die spiritually. Without Christ, you already are dead spiritually, but he wants to revive your spirit and give you new life.

How can you be born again? Go back to being like a child. Humble yourself and leave everything at Jesus' feet, giving him control of your life. You're sick of your sin, but Jesus forgives you, and you start all over again, as a new person. Now you want to know Christ and walk with him.

The person born of the Spirit is like the wind

8 The wind blows wherever it pleases. You hear its sound, but you cannot tell where it comes from or where it is going. So it is with everyone born of the Spirit."

There is something mysterious, difficult to grasp, about the person born of the Spirit. They don't walk according to the ways of this world. They may look different than most people and feel misunderstood. We want to know where we came from and where we're going; we want to know everything, but part of humbling yourself is admitting that you don't know everything. You no longer run your life; Jesus does. He guides you.

9 Nicodemus asked, "What do you mean by this? How does this happen?" (MSG)

Wow! It appears that Nicodemus was beginning to grasp what Jesus was saying. He wanted to know how it happens. But Jesus didn't say, "Great! For it to happen, all you have to do is pray this prayer." Jesus always speaks the truth; he is not afraid of offending anyone, and he is in no hurry to notch another "conversion," even if it is someone as important as this Pharisee.

10 "You are Israel's teacher," said Jesus, "and do you not understand these things?11 Very truly I tell you, we speak of what we know, and we testify to what we have seen, but still you people do not accept our testimony. 12 I have spoken to you of earthly things and you do not believe; how then will you believe if I speak of heavenly things?

Jesus expects a religious teacher, someone with extensive knowledge of the Bible, to be familiar with these things; however, even today, there are teachers in the church who don't understand spiritual truth. Much of Jesus' teaching pertained to daily life, which was difficult for many people to accept. There were deeper teachings Jesus wanted to share with them—heavenly things—but he knew they couldn't receive them.

Jesus spoke about what he knew, what he had seen in heaven. How can you tell if you should receive someone's teaching?

- Study the fruit of their lives: Do they reflect Jesus? Do they walk in the truth, in love, and righteousness?
- Do they speak from the Bible?
- Do they glorify God?
- Does God's Spirit within you confirm that it is the truth?

Jesus must be lifted up

[13] No one has ever gone into heaven except the one who came from heaven—the Son of Man.[14] Just as Moses lifted up the snake in the wilderness, so the Son of Man must be lifted up, [15] that everyone who believes may have eternal life in him."

Now Jesus revealed himself to Nicodemus:

- Jesus came from heaven. There is a heaven, a spiritual dimension on an entirely different level than this universe, and Jesus came from that heaven to live here on earth.
- It is possible to have eternal life and enter that heaven.
- The offer is open to anyone who believes in Jesus. The one who doesn't believe is lost.

The key to this is something radical, something that Jesus has shared with very few people: He must be lifted up. I doubt if Nicodemus understood what that meant. For many, the cross was a disgrace: How could God allow his beloved son to suffer the cruelest death possible? Only a perfect sacrifice would be able to pay the price of our sins, but that doesn't make sense to most people.

Jesus compared it to an unusual event that occurred during the Exodus (Num. 21:4–9). Once again, the people were complaining. God had had enough of their complaints and sent snakes to bite them. When Moses called out to God, the Lord told him to make a bronze snake and lift it up. Everyone who looked at the snake would be healed. How strange that to bring healing, God would use a symbol of the very creature that tempted Eve in Eden!

God so loved the world

[16] *For God so loved the world that he gave his one and only Son, that whoever believes in him shall not perish but have eternal life.*

Everyone is going to live forever. Jesus is talking here about a life of blessing for all eternity; the alternative is an eternity in hell, lost. It could be that you are already in a living hell. Jesus came to save you and give you a full and abundant life now, and eternal life with him in heaven. Do you have that hope? If you have accepted Jesus, do you have the assurance that Christ is preparing a place for you in heaven, and someday you will see him face to face?

God loves you. That is hard to grasp if you have never experienced genuine love. Many think of God as a judge, ready to punish them for the least infraction. They may have had an abusive father who was constantly beating and punishing them. Unfortunately, many have experienced the condemnation of a pastor or priest, fellow church members, or a Christian father. The proof of God's love is what he gave us: salvation, and his only Son. That is true love.

Jesus didn't come to condemn the world

¹⁷ For God did not send his Son into the world to condemn the world, but to save the world through him.

There is a coming judgment. The next verse tells us that many have already been condemned, but not by Jesus; he didn't come to condemn, but to save. He paid the price for every wrong you have committed, and wants to free you from guilt and give you a new life.

¹⁸ Whoever believes in him is not condemned, but whoever does not believe stands condemned already because they have not believed in the name of God's one and only Son.

There are only two options: to be saved, or be condemned. Do you believe there are many paths to God? Jesus said: *"I am the way, the truth, and the life. No one comes to the Father but by me"* (Jn. 14:6). The only way to be saved and see God's kingdom is to believe in the name of Jesus. What does that mean? In the Bible, a name represents everything a person is and stands for. To believe in Jesus' name is to believe he is God's only Son, who came to this world as a man, walked among us, and lived a perfect life. He died on the cross and rose again to pay the price of your sin, and is coming again to establish his kingdom.

If you choose not to give your life to Jesus or believe in him, you already stand condemned. God doesn't condemn anyone; they are condemned by the sin and rebellion that is part of our nature. God went to the extreme of sending his own Son to die on the cross and save us from that condemnation.

Six times in this chapter, Jesus speaks of belief or having faith. Hebrews 11:1 says that faith is the assurance of what we hope for and the certainty of what is not seen. Faith comes by hearing, and hearing by the Word of God. Read the Gospel of Mark, for example. Reading about what Jesus did, God will confirm that it is true, and your faith will grow.

Do you love the darkness?

[19] This is the verdict: Light has come into the world, but people loved darkness instead of light because their deeds were evil.[20] Everyone who does evil hates the light, and will not come into the light for fear that their deeds will be exposed.

Which do you love more? The light? Or darkness? Are you attracted by things that are dirty and corrupt? Are you afraid of the light? How are your works? We are not condemned by God, but by the decisions we make. Many people know that they could come to the light, come to Christ, and be saved, but don't want to leave the parties, the women, and their life in the darkness. Some young people say: "I want to enjoy life now; maybe when I'm older I'll accept Jesus."

The person who walks in darkness fears the light. They know they're wrong and want to hide what they're doing. They click off the porn when their wife comes home or delete the chat when their husband enters the room. They hide what they're stealing from their job. They prefer the darkness of the bar, and people who won't look down on them for their sin and adultery. That is why they may hate the Christian who walks in holiness; they fear that their deeds will be exposed. You may be able to deceive your spouse or boss, but you can't fool God.

Is it really worth losing your family, your job, and maybe your life, because you love the darkness? The person who walks in darkness is a slave to it. It is liberating to walk in the light, free from sin, enjoying life in God's kingdom of righteousness and peace. You will feel so much better. I invite you to come to the light right now.

Everything exposed by the light

²¹ But whoever lives by the truth comes into the light, so that it may be seen plainly that what they have done has been done in the sight of God.

It is so beautiful to walk transparently, with nothing to hide, with a pure heart. You may have served God in secret; nobody knows the good works you have done. The same may be true of your sin. The Bible says all our works will be shouted from the rooftops. Everyone will know.

On another occasion, Jesus said:

There is nothing concealed that will not be disclosed, or hidden that will not be made known. What you have said in the dark will be heard in the daylight, and what you have whispered in the ear in the inner rooms will be proclaimed from the roofs.

"I tell you, my friends, do not be afraid of those who kill the body and after that can do no more. But I will show you whom you should fear: Fear him who, after your body has been killed, has authority to throw you into hell. Yes, I tell you, fear him. Are not five sparrows sold for two pennies? Yet not one of them is forgotten by God. Indeed, the very hairs of your head are all numbered. Don't be afraid; you are worth more than many sparrows.

"I tell you, whoever publicly acknowledges me before others, the Son of Man will also acknowledge before the angels of God. But whoever disowns me before others will be disowned before the angels of God (Lk. 12:2–9).

We don't know if Nicodemus was born again that night, if he repented and entered God's kingdom. But he did believe in Jesus; when Christ died on the cross Nicodemus brought myrrh and aloe to anoint his body, and, together with Joseph of Arimathea, placed his body in the tomb.

You can make the most important decision of your life. You can be born again, start a new life, and live eternally in God's kingdom. If you are already in his kingdom, you can walk as Jesus walked, and share this message with others, inviting them to come into his kingdom.

3

How to Stay Close to Jesus

John 15:1–10

You have had the chance to enter through the small door and evaluate the cost of being Jesus' disciple. It is such a radical change that Jesus says the only way to make it is to start all over and be born again. Rehabilitation won't work; we have to crucify the old self and begin again with a child-like faith. You're still reading this book; apparently, you still want to walk with Jesus on the narrow road, like our key verse says (1 Jn. 2:5–6):

By this we may be sure that we are in [Christ]: whoever says, 'I abide in him', ought to walk just as he walked.

We don't just want to *say* we're abiding in or remaining in Christ, we want to really do it. The word "abide" is the same word John used in Chapter 15 of his Gospel. The NIV uses the more common word "remain" instead of "abide":

*⁴ **Remain** in me, as I also **remain** in you. No branch can bear fruit by itself; it must **remain** in the vine. Neither can you bear fruit unless you **remain** in me.*

*⁵ "I am the vine; you are the branches. If you **remain** in me and I in you, you will bear much fruit; apart from me you can do nothing. ⁶ If you do not **remain** in me, you are like a branch that is thrown away and withers; such branches are picked up, thrown* *into the fire and burned.* ⁷*If you* **remain** *in me and my words* **remain** *in you, ask whatever you wish, and it will be done for you.* ⁸*This is to my Father's glory, that you bear much fruit, showing yourselves to be my disciples.*

⁹*"As the Father has loved me, so have I loved you. Now* **remain** *in my love.* ¹⁰*If you keep my commands, you will* **remain** *in my love, just as I have kept my Father's commands and* **remain** *in his love.*

These are the key points of this passage, which we will explore in this chapter:

- We must remain in Christ, and he wants to remain in us (although there are some conditions for that).

- Christ remains in God's love, and his words must remain in us.

- To remain in him is not optional, for only a few super-spiritual believers. The person who does not remain in him is cast into the fire and burned.

- The secret of answered prayer is remaining in Christ.

- The key to a fruitful life is remaining in Christ.

- To remain in Christ, we must keep his commandments.

How is it going for you? Would you say you are abiding in Christ? Are you walking as Jesus walked? Be honest. That is the first step. You can't deceive God. If Jesus lives in you and you keep his word, you will walk as he walked. He has given you his Spirit to guide and empower you.

God wants you to be fruitful

[1] *"I am the true vine, and my Father is the gardener.* [2] *He cuts off every branch in me that bears no fruit, while every branch that does bear fruit he prunes so that it will be even more fruitful.*

Jesus is the only true vine, and we are the branches in that vine, connected and united to him. We are an integral part of the vine; one cannot exist without the other. Without branches, the vine is useless; it can't bear fruit. It is the branches that produce fruit. Without the vine, the branches die; you receive everything you need from the vine. You also need the other branches; God connects you to the vine, one branch among many. The primary purpose of your salvation is to produce the best fruit possible in significant quantities. It is not to make your life easier, or to prosper you in your job, or to be happy and blessed. Those things may happen, but that is not God's principal purpose for you.

Examining the condition of the branches

Jesus finished his work here on earth; he did everything necessary to provide many branches for his Father's vine. The Father is the gardener; it is his vineyard, and he is always at work, examining the branches. He has every right to do what he wants to in his vineyard. He is looking at your life right now. Is it fruitful? If your branch is not fruitful, he will cut it off. That is what it says, isn't it? A fruitless branch serves no purpose for the Lord; it simply takes energy away from the fruitful branches. The lovely green leaves and beautiful flowers don't matter; he wants fruit.

Now, don't get scared. There is time before the harvest; you can still make some changes to be more fruitful. The Father is patient with you. He knows that the vine has to grow and be able to bear fruit, just as a girl must grow up before bearing a child. The Father is an expert gardener, and will do everything possible and necessary to assure a good harvest, even if it is radical.

Pruning

It could be that the Father is pruning you right now. It is a tough process, and it hurts. You may ask: "Why is this happening to me? I've been working hard. I'm seeking God, and I have seen some good fruit in my life." But the Father wants more. It is actually good if you are being pruned; it means he has something greater for you.

What fruit is he looking for?

It begins with the fruit of the Spirit in Galatians 5:22–23: *love, joy, peace, forbearance, kindness, goodness, faithfulness, gentleness and self-control.* Those are important, but God is also looking for fruit in other people whom you have impacted, those who have received Christ, are growing in the Lord, and are serving God: "*No good tree bears bad fruit, nor does a bad tree bear good fruit. Each tree is recognized by its own fruit. People do not pick figs from thornbushes, or grapes from briers. A good man brings good things out of the good stored up in his heart, and an evil man brings evil things out of the evil stored up in his heart. For the mouth speaks what the heart is full of* (Lk. 6:43–45)."

What is in your heart? What is stored up there? Your words reveal the state of your heart. Are they harsh and ugly? Hard words? Or do you speak to build up and bless others?

³ You are already clean because of the word I have spoken to you.

How does the Father cleanse, or prune, you? With the Word: *For the word of God is alive and active. Sharper than any double-edged sword, it penetrates even to dividing soul and spirit, joints and marrow; it judges the thoughts and attitudes of the heart*

(Heb. 4:12). You have to be in the Word, and let the Holy Spirit cleanse and prune you with his Word. God also uses other people, trials, and life's circumstances to prune you.

What is the secret of a fruitful life?

⁴ Remain in me, as I also remain in you. No branch can bear fruit by itself; it must remain in the vine. Neither can you bear fruit unless you remain in me.

The key words in these ten verses are "remain" (or abide, which appears ten times) and "fruit" (six times). It is common sense: No branch that has been cut from a tree or vine can bear fruit. You have to remain united to Christ, to the vine. The question for you, then, is: Are you remaining in Christ? Can you say with confidence that he abides in you? How can you know?

A church can have anointed services and offer impressive programs. It may have a beautiful building and great music, and people who are hard at work, but those things don't necessarily mean success. The test is the fruit. It is possible to do a lot of religious things in your own strength, in the flesh, but the only way to bear fruit that lasts is to remain united to Christ.

⁵ "I am the vine; you are the branches. If you remain in me and I in you, you will bear much fruit; apart from me you can do nothing.

It is interesting that Jesus gave this teaching to the eleven disciples that night in the Upper Room. Soon they would be physically separated from Jesus. They had spent three years in close fellowship with him, being prepared for the ministry. It is common for a Christian to feel God's presence in the first months after conversion, but just as those disciples had to learn to stay united to him without his physical presence, you may go through times when you don't feel his presence—a dark night. You must learn not to rely solely on feelings. It is called faith; faith that Christ lives in you and your life is in Christ.

God wants a lot of fruit from you, but the quality is just as important as the quantity. God is not pleased with a ton of rotten fruit. Just as a healthy tree produces large amounts of good fruit, so a healthy Christian should produce much good fruit. That is a promise, but as with most promises, there is a condition: Remain in Christ and Christ in you. Then you can be sure you will produce much good fruit.

⁶ If you do not remain in me, you are like a branch that is thrown away and withers; such branches are picked up, thrown into the fire and burned.

There it is again; Jesus repeats that it is possible to end up in the fire. Abiding in Christ is not optional, as though there are some mature Christians who remain in Christ and others who only come to him when they need something. They drink some living water during the church service and go back to the world during the week. Jesus has some very strong words for those who do not remain in him. He is always faithful to do his part in sustaining us and sharing his life with us, but you must remain in him. You can decide not to remain in him, or more commonly, simply neglect your relationship with him.

The second promise

⁷ If you remain in me and my words remain in you, ask whatever you wish, and it will be done for you.

The first promise is to bear much fruit if you remain in Jesus. Now he slightly changes the condition: This promise is for the person who remains in Jesus, and Jesus' words remain in him. That is a great promise, but it is not for selfish requests; it is given in the context of your work in the vine. Of course, God wants to provide your needs, but he particularly wants to answer prayers that will help in your fruitfulness. If his Word truly remains in you, you will have his heart, and ask according to his will.

⁸ This is to my Father's glory, that you bear much fruit, showing yourselves to be my disciples.

Are you Jesus' disciple? A disciple is fruitful, and God desires a great deal of fruit. Do you want to glorify God? Don't you think God will be pleased with you if you glorify him in this way?

⁹ "As the Father has loved me, so have I loved you. Now remain in my love.

It is not just a matter of being fruitful and working in the vineyard; it is a love relationship, and it is a command: Remain in Jesus' love. He loves you with the same love the Father has for him. That is amazing love! That love is always there for you. In this chapter, when Jesus speaks of love, he uses the word *agape*, God's unconditional and perfect love. You can depend on his love, but you have to remain in it. How?

¹⁰ If you keep my commands, you will remain in my love, just as I have kept my Father's commands and remain in his love.

So, how do you remain in Christ, and remain in his love?

- Obey his commands.
- Stay in fellowship with him.
- Walk with him throughout the day, in worship and prayer.
- Walk in holiness; you cannot remain in Christ while you are remaining in your sin.

What a great privilege: To live united to Christ and bear much fruit for the glory of his name. Studying his life and walking as he walked, as we learn in this book, you will remain in him, and his love will remain in you.

4

Resisting Temptation

Luke 4:1–14

No way! I have just decided to get on the narrow road and leave everything to walk with Jesus. Now you're telling me I have an enemy who is going to tempt me to get back on the broad path? I have to learn how to fight? Yep, I'm afraid that's the way it is. Before Jesus began his ministry, he had to pass a rigorous test: forty days of temptation, face-to-face with the devil. He resisted all those temptations, but it wasn't the end of the tests; he was tempted throughout his life. It could be that you have fallen, and the devil is taunting you: "You will never be a good Christian." Right here, at the beginning of this new walk with Jesus, you may be tempted to give up and throw in the towel. A crucial aspect of your growth is exercising your faith in spiritual battles, just as we lift weights to develop physically. Learning to recognize, resist, and defeat temptation is a start.

If you are neglecting your spiritual life, there will be more temptation, although when you're far from God, you may not even be aware of it. Walking close to Jesus, full of the Spirit, you are less apt to fall into temptation, but this portion shows that you are not exempt. In fact, at times, the fiercest temptations come after a great spiritual experience. In Jesus' case, it was right after his baptism in water and the Spirit.

¹Jesus, full of the Holy Spirit, left the Jordan and was led by the Spirit into the wilderness.

We pray that God would "lead us not into temptation" in the Lord's Prayer, but Jesus was led by the Spirit to the place of temptation, to the wilderness. Are you in a wilderness? Whether God sent you there for a purpose, or you're there as a result of your rebellion, temptation is part of life in the wilderness.

Where does temptation come from?

Not from God; he never tempts us, but he can allow temptation.

When tempted, no one should say, "God is tempting me." For God cannot be tempted by evil, nor does he tempt anyone; but each person is tempted when they are dragged away by their own evil desire and enticed. Then, after desire has conceived, it gives birth to sin; and sin, when it is full-grown, gives birth to death (Jas. 1:13–15).

Temptation has three sources:

1. Your evil desires, which entice you. Examine your desires, avoid those situations where you are most apt to be enticed, and reject your fleshly desires before they give birth to sinful acts. Learn to recognize temptation. Not all desire is evil. God has given all of us fleshly desires—the question is how we handle them, to satisfy them in a way that is pleasing to God. If the "carnal" man wants to see porn, he goes to that app on his phone without thinking twice. The spiritual man recognizes it as temptation, which can lead to sin that will break his communion with God and ultimately end in death. Instead of giving in, say to the Lord: "I'm tempted to see porn. Help me not to be enticed by that temptation."

2. People and things in the world. Avoid those friends, places, TV programs, and internet sites that drag you away and entice you to sin. You can avoid many worldly temptations if you genuinely want to. If a friend offers you a chance to make some fast (dirty) money, there should be a red light: Temptation! I need to get out of here! If you're an alcoholic and a friend invites you to a bar, be careful!

3. For Jesus, it was the devil, but it's usually not this obvious for us. Satan walks around like a roaring lion—but often in sheep's clothing—looking for someone to tempt and devour. Nobody is exempt; it could be that lonely, weak, backslidden sheep, or the Son of God.

40 days of temptations

²For forty days he was tempted by the devil. He ate nothing during those days, and at the end of them he was hungry.

Traditionally, many have taught that Jesus spent forty days fasting, with some temptations at the end, but the best translation of the Greek suggests that he was tempted the entire forty days—only the final (and toughest) temptations are recorded. Many times the devil tries to entice with the same temptation day after day. The first day is easy; you come out of church full of the Spirit and easily reject the temptation. But after several weeks of Satan presenting you with the same image (almost like virtual reality!), you get tired, and in a moment of discouragement and weakness, you fall. Stand firm in your faith and in the Spirit! Keep on resisting!

If you are in a season of intense temptation, consider a fast to spiritually strengthen yourself. The fast gave Jesus more spiritual strength, but also left him more vulnerable to the temptation of bread. Jesus was alone—except for the powerful communion of the Father and the Holy Spirit! Temptation is almost always stronger when we are alone. Remember that God is there 24/7. You can also send a message to a trusted friend, sharing the temptation and asking for prayer. If possible, leave your lonely house to take a walk or visit someone.

It's easy to feel discouraged by the intensity of the temptations and feel like you're in sin or a bad Christian. Temptation is not sin! Don't get down because the temptations are so perverse!

The first temptation: Satisfying the desire of your flesh

³ *The devil said to him, "If you are the Son of God, tell this stone to become bread."*

The first temptation appears innocent. God provided bread (manna) for the Hebrews in the wilderness. Later, Jesus would multiply bread to feed multitudes. Eating bread is not sinful. We can rationalize that a temptation is not bad, but no matter how legitimate it may look, never obey the devil!

What was the nature of this temptation?

- Questioning your relationship to God, tempting you to defend yourself and do something wrong to show others your spiritual power and connection with God. The word translated "If" can also be "given that." It could be that the devil didn't doubt that Jesus was God's Son; he knew Jesus could do it, but also knew it would be a sin to use his power to satisfy his own needs.

- Doing something to satisfy your fleshly appetites, whether it is illicit sex or something that looks innocent, like bread. It can mean not waiting for God's time (for something good), trying to speed up God's plan in your own strength. For example, sex in marriage is a great blessing, but it is a powerful temptation to have sex before marriage.

- Jesus' word had the power to create the universe and raise the dead, and there is great power in the word we proclaim in Jesus' name. We must be sure that we speak according to God's will.

Many times Satan sows a seed with a temptation. At that time, strengthened by his fast and knowing that the temptation came from the devil, Jesus could resist. But on another occasion, when he was hungry and alone, that seed could give birth: "I did create the universe by my word. Forget bread! I can speak a tasty steak into existence!" Of course, that wouldn't happen with Jesus, but we must not provide the seed with a favorable environment to germinate. Be ever vigilant, and try to destroy that seed.

In this case, it was just a thought, but many times that is enough to drag us away. The temptation is even stronger if you can smell or taste the freshly baked bread!

It is written

[4] *Jesus answered, "It is written: 'Man shall not live on bread alone, but by every word of God.'"*

In each case Jesus neither argued with the devil nor rebuked him; he simply declared what the Word of God says (here he cited Deuteronomy 8:3). You have to study and memorize the Word, so that it remains in you. In the heat of temptation, you probably won't have time to look up a verse on your phone or in your Bible—that Word must be hidden in your heart. God's Word is your bread, your life, and your sword (Eph. 6:17)—not only some promises or favorite verses, but *every* word.

Jesus never contemplated doing what the devil wanted. If you start to evaluate the possibilities and consequences of something that comes from the evil one, it will be easy to fall into his temptation. If there is any doubt, it is better to say "no" from the start.

Satan didn't try to convince Jesus or question God's word; he just changed his tactic.

The second temptation: fame, power, and glory

⁵ The devil led him up to a high place and showed him in an instant all the kingdoms of the world. ⁶ And he said to him, "I will give you all their authority and splendor; it has been given to me, and I can give it to anyone I want to. ⁷ If you worship me, it will all be yours."

Is it possible that just as the Spirit led Jesus into the wilderness, the devil physically led him to this high place? Could be. This time the devil is wiser, and *shows* him the kingdoms. Men respond strongly to what they *see*.

This was a temptation to take the easy road to riches, power, and fame. It's very bold for the devil to ask Jesus to bow down and worship him, but when someone offers a man power and fame, he can do foolish things. Jesus knows that the Father has promised him a kingdom—not only in this world, but the whole universe!—and all power, but this would be a way to avoid the agony of the cross. Jesus commands us to take up our cross and follow him, crucifying the old man and its desires. Nobody— including Jesus—wants to be crucified. The devil will tempt us to avoid the hard work and pain of doing things God's way. We also are going to inherit a kingdom in the future; the temptation is to get impatient and try to claim it ahead of time. Could it be that Satan is trying to hinder God's purpose for your life?

Is it true that the kingdoms of this world have been given to Satan, and he can give them to anyone he wants to? To some extent. Could it be that Satan has given someone a kingdom in the world today?

Worship and serve God alone

⁸ Jesus answered, "Get behind me, Satan. It is written: 'Worship the Lord your God and serve him only.'" (Citing Deuteronomy 6:13)

Jesus has had enough! Worship an angel that he created? That is ridiculous! It's okay to tell the devil to go away.

Satan can offer the world and its pleasures to us, but there is a very high—and eternal—cost involved in worshipping and serving him! The temptation of the fast track to wealth, power, and fame is strong. We might never think of bowing down to the devil, but even if you don't bow down to him, are you really worshipping God? It is more than singing some songs in church; it is a lifestyle, a life of service to God. If we spend more time with perverse things on TV and the internet than we do serving God and in his presence, is it possible we are really worshipping the devil? Jesus said, *"serve him only."* Who are you serving? Even your secular work should be done as unto the Lord.

The third temptation: Twist the Scriptures and tempt God

⁹ The devil led him to Jerusalem and had him stand on the highest point of the temple. "If you are the Son of God," he said, "throw yourself down from here. ¹⁰ For it is written:

"'He will command his angels concerning you
*   to guard you carefully;*
¹¹ they will lift you up in their hands,
*   so that you will not strike your foot against a stone.'"*

Satan knows the Bible, and distorts it for his own purposes. Here he cites Psalm 91:11–12. It is one thing to take verses from the Bible—often out of context—or even have extensive biblical knowledge; it's another thing to obey it and walk according to the spirit of the Word. Here is another "journey," this time to the holy city, to the temple, the very center of the worship of the living God. Again, we don't know if they were physically in Jerusalem, with all the people able to see them on the pinnacle of the temple, or if they were there spiritually. Do you think Satan goes to church? Definitely!

There are various temptations here, among them suicide. Would God allow Jesus to die if he threw himself off the temple to prove he was God's Son? We don't know, but Satan may have thought Jesus would die. He also touched human pride and our tendency to exalt ourselves. God is not our magician in the sky, and we always have to resist foolish tests of his power and word.

Don't put God to the test

¹² Jesus answered, "It is said: 'Do not put the Lord your God to the test.'"

Jesus was not impressed with Satan's biblical knowledge. This time Jesus didn't say "it is written," but rather "it is said," still referring to the Scripture (Deut. 6:16). This could be understood two ways:

1. Jesus would be tempting his Father if he were to do something presumptuous to prove himself to Satan and see if God would rescue him

2. Jesus is speaking directly to Satan, saying: "Enough already. I am the Lord, your God. You are forbidden to test me."

Don't play with God or try to manipulate him!

Jesus was tempted in everything, just like you!

This experience equipped Jesus to understand your struggle with temptation. For all eternity, he had never been tempted! These were real temptations, with the very real possibility of sinning, and this was not the only time he was tempted:

Therefore, since we have a great high priest who has ascended into heaven, Jesus the Son of God, let us hold firmly to the faith we profess. For we do not have a high priest who is unable to empathize with our weaknesses, but we have one who has been tempted in every way, just as we are—yet he did not sin. Let us then approach God's throne of grace with confidence, so that we may receive mercy and find grace to help us in our time of need (Heb. 4:14–16).

Here are four important things to help you in temptation:

- You have a high priest who is interceding for you right now. He is for you, and holds you up with his intercession when you are going through trials.

- Stand firm in your faith. Declare what the Word of God says about who you are and what Christ has done for you.

- Your temptation is not unique; Jesus was tempted in every way just as you are.

- Draw close to God in prayer; there you will find mercy and grace to help you in the toughest moments of temptation.

For this reason he had to be made like them, fully human in every way, in order that he might become a merciful and faithful high priest in service to God, and that he might make atonement for the sins of the people. Because he himself suffered when he was tempted, he is able to help those who are being tempted (Heb. 2:17–18).

An important verse to memorize

No temptation has overtaken you except what is common to mankind. And God is faithful; he will not let you be tempted beyond what you can bear. But when you are tempted, he will also provide a way out so that you can endure it (1 Cor. 10:13).

Keep this verse in your mind, and remember these truths:

- Satan has many years observing our race and knows very well which temptations are most likely to make us fall.

- God is faithful in the midst of temptation.

- God is Lord of the temptations; he allows only what he knows you are able to withstand.

- No matter how strong the current temptation, you can stand up under it.

- In the midst of every temptation, God will show you a way out. There is *always* a way out. You are *never* forced to fall in the temptation, but *you* have to resist it and ask God for that way out. The sad reality is that often we *want* to fall in the temptation.

When Jesus prayed in anguish in Gethsemane, he told his disciples:

"Watch and pray so that you will not fall into temptation. The spirit is willing, but the flesh is weak" (Matt. 26:41).

The end of the temptation

13 When the devil had finished all this tempting, he left him until an opportune time.

Matthew adds (4:11): *Then the devil left him, and angels came and attended him.*

There will be times of intense temptation. We may give in to them and spend years in the wilderness, instead of forty days. But if we resist the temptation, the devil has to flee (Jms. 4:7). He will leave you for a while, and you may experience a rest from his attacks, but he will return.

You may be tempted by something your whole life. For example, if porn was a problem for you in the past, it may always be a strong temptation. For another man, it could be alcohol. Satan observes us and tempts us according to our weaknesses and what enticed us in the past. Don't worry when that happens. Recognize it as a temptation, say "no," and keep going. With time and increased spiritual maturity, temptations often become more subtle; be prepared for them.

God is watching the whole process. He may allow the devil to test you for a while, but he will never leave you. And when you pass the test, just like Jesus, he may send angels (or other Christians) to minister to you.

14 Jesus returned to Galilee in the power of the Spirit, and news about him spread through the whole countryside.

Jesus started these forty days full of the Spirit. He was severely tempted and tested. I'm sure there were times during the fast, hungry, and face to face with the devil, that he didn't feel much of the Spirit's presence. That is one of the temptations we face: Unbelief, thinking that God has left me, and I'm never going to get out of this wilderness. Yes, Jesus was tempted in everything just like you and me. If you are in a wilderness right now and are tempted to believe the devil's lies, be strong and courageous, because if you stand firm in your faith, the day will come when you leave the wilderness and return in the power of the Spirit to your family, ministry, and walk with the Lord.

Adam, the first man, was tempted and failed the test. The second Adam, Jesus, passed the test and was ready to begin his public ministry. Jesus never sought publicity; in fact, he almost always asked the people he healed or delivered to stay quiet, but his fame still spread throughout the whole region.

Patiently endure the trials and temptations!

Blessed is the one who perseveres under trials and temptations because, having stood the test, that person will receive the crown of life that the Lord has promised to those who love him (Jms. 1:12).

Temptation, trial, and test all come from the same Greek word. Temptations are tests which reveal how serious we are about resisting sin and the devil. No temptation or trial is pleasant, but just as we have seen in Jesus' life, there is a great reward after overcoming. The advice here is to patiently endure them. Neither "patience" nor "endure" sounds pleasant, but when we have stood the test, God has a crown of life awaiting us.

Which temptations are strongest for you right now? How are you doing in resisting them? Could it be that God has allowed Satan to tempt you and test you in preparation for something greater that the Lord has for you?

5

Fill Your Empty Jars to the Brim!

John 2:1–11

Jesus has called you to leave everything, be born again, and follow him as his disciple on the narrow road. We saw in the last chapter that there are temptations, trials, and warfare on that road; now we're going to take a break for a moment. Jesus also knows how to have fun! John Chapter 2 flows directly out of the first chapter with these words: *"On the third day."* We are at the very beginning of Jesus' ministry, right after his temptations. The first day John the Baptist presented Jesus as the Messiah, and the second day Jesus called his first disciples. They—perhaps like you—were just beginning to learn what life was like walking with Jesus.

¹On the third day a wedding took place at Cana in Galilee. Jesus' mother was there, ² and Jesus and his disciples had also been invited to the wedding.

Cana was about eight miles (13.5 km) from Nazareth. The couple may have been friends or relatives of Jesus' family. Joseph is never mentioned in any context during Jesus' ministry; we don't know when, but he had already died. It is interesting that God would allow Jesus to lose his earthly father at a young age.

When we walk as Jesus walked, we take part in family occasions

A wedding may not appear very spiritual, but it celebrates something foundational to our race, instituted by God: the union of a man and woman to become one flesh and produce godly offspring. A wedding was a big celebration, and the Jews knew how to throw a party. Wine played a significant role and may have been the only beverage. How sad that some Christians are so serious they barely know how to laugh and celebrate! Some hesitate to take part in family gatherings because "they're not saved," and alcohol and worldly music will be involved. They are great opportunities to show by our lives how wonderful it is to walk with the Lord. Jesus' example was to participate enthusiastically, but without sinning. When you receive an invitation, pray about it before deciding whether to accept or decline. Of course, God knows your family situation and spiritual strength, and sometimes it may be better not to go.

When we walk as Jesus walked, we honor marriage

Who would imagine that Jesus would perform his first miracle at a wedding, and do something that doesn't seem very important? Nobody was saved, healed, or delivered. But in God's plan, his Son did his first miracle on earth at a wedding, and in so doing affirmed the sanctity and importance of marriage. How tragic that many people (including Christians) are avoiding marriage, feeling that the commitment is not that important. Even worse, men are marrying men and women marrying women.

Jesus' wedding

Was it hard for Jesus to go to a wedding, knowing that he would never marry? Possibly, but he already was planning the most impressive wedding in history, and that day in Cana he was probably thinking about it. Just like any bridegroom, he is anxious for that day to arrive, but he has to wait on his Father's timing. The Father wants as many as possible at that wedding; he wants heaven full.

If you are Jesus' disciple, you are invited to his wedding. In fact, you are the bride; the whole church, every believer, is the bride of Christ. But to get into the wedding, you are going to need wedding clothes:

"But when the king came in to see the guests, he noticed a man there who was not wearing wedding clothes. He asked, 'How did you get in here without wedding clothes, friend?' The man was speechless.

"Then the king told the attendants, 'Tie him hand and foot, and throw him outside, into the darkness, where there will be weeping and gnashing of teeth.' "For many are invited, but few are chosen." (Matt. 22:11-14)

Everyone is invited to this wedding. Amazingly, many who are invited don't want to go:

Jesus spoke to them again in parables, saying: "The kingdom of heaven is like a king who prepared a wedding banquet for his son. He sent his servants to those who had been invited to the banquet to tell them to come, but they refused to come.

"Then he sent some more servants and said, 'Tell those who have been invited that I have prepared my dinner: My oxen and

fattened cattle have been butchered, and everything is ready. Come to the wedding banquet.'

"But they paid no attention and went off—one to his field, another to his business. The rest seized his servants, mistreated them and killed them. The king was enraged. He sent his army and destroyed those murderers and burned their city.

"Then he said to his servants, 'The wedding banquet is ready, but those I invited did not deserve to come. So go to the street corners and invite to the banquet anyone you find.' So the servants went out into the streets and gathered all the people they could find, the bad as well as the good, and the wedding hall was filled with guests (Matt. 22:1-10).

The chosen are those who waited for the call to the wedding, are excited when the call comes, and carefully dress in appropriate wedding clothes. Jesus gives you those clothes when you accept him as Lord and Savior, yet tragically, many will show up at the wedding without the right clothes, and will be tied up and thrown out to a place of weeping and gnashing of teeth. Do you have the right clothes? The first two chapters of this book show you how to be saved and receive those clothes. Are you walking in holiness? This book teaches you to walk as Jesus walked. Do you have the assurance that God has chosen you? The fact that you are reading this book shows that God has chosen you and is calling you to walk with him.

In John's Gospel, on the first day, John the Baptist proclaimed Jesus as the Lamb of God; on the second day, Jesus called his first disciples; and now, on the third day, he is at this wedding. In the broader context, on the first day, Jesus was proclaimed as Savior and Messiah. On the second day—right now—he is calling and preparing his disciples. We are awaiting the third day, when he returns for his wedding.

Then I heard what sounded like a great multitude, like the roar of rushing waters and like loud peals of thunder, shouting:

"Hallelujah!
For our Lord God Almighty reigns.
Let us rejoice and be glad
and give him glory!
For the wedding of the Lamb has come,
and his bride has made herself ready.
Fine linen, bright and clean,
was given her to wear."

(Fine linen stands for the righteous acts of God's holy people.)

Then the angel said to me, "Write this: Blessed are those who are invited to the wedding supper of the Lamb!" And he added, "These are the true words of God."

(Rev. 19:6–9)

What a day that will be! Will you be there? And your family? What do you need to do to prepare for the wedding?

The fruit of the vine

³ When the wine was gone, Jesus' mother said to him, "They have no more wine."

They had been drinking a lot. It is not the purpose of this study to enter into the controversy surrounding wine in the Bible: was it alcoholic or not? It is clear that many times when the Bible speaks of wine, it contained alcohol—hence the prohibition on getting drunk with wine (Eph. 5:18).

The last time Jesus drank wine was the night of his arrest. He is waiting for his wedding to drink wine again. That night in the Upper Room, he said to his disciples:

"I have eagerly desired to eat this Passover with you before I suffer. For I tell you, I will not eat it again until it finds fulfillment in the kingdom of God."

After taking the cup, he gave thanks and said, "Take this and divide it among you. For I tell you I will not drink again from the fruit of the vine until the kingdom of God comes."

And he took bread, gave thanks and broke it, and gave it to them, saying, "This is my body given for you; do this in remembrance of me."

In the same way, after the supper he took the cup, saying, "This cup is the new covenant in my blood, which is poured out for you (Lk. 22:15–20).

When we partake of the Lord's Supper, we affirm our commitment to that covenant, remembering Christ's sacrifice on the cross, and looking forward to his wedding feast, when the kingdom of God comes and he drinks wine again.

The importance of planning

Mary had already learned that when there was a problem, Jesus could solve it. A mother can be manipulative, and Mary was not beyond manipulating her son. I'm sure she did it with the best of intentions, but she didn't understand the implications of what she said. She knew that this recently married couple (and their families) were in trouble. We don't know if they had failed to buy enough wine, or if the guests drank too much. You may be aware that in the world, it can still be a significant issue if the beer or alcohol runs out at a wedding. They weren't drinking to get drunk, but the wine was important.

The failure was a result of a lack of planning, a common problem for individuals and churches. Of course, we must be guided by the Holy Spirit and entrust our future to the Lord, who can change our plans if he so desires. But there are many examples of planning in the Bible, including planning for this wedding of the Lamb:

"At that time the kingdom of heaven will be like ten virgins who took their lamps and went out to meet the bridegroom. Five of them were foolish and five were wise. The foolish ones took their lamps but did not take any oil with them. The wise ones, however, took oil in jars along with their lamps. The bridegroom was a long time in coming, and they all became drowsy and fell asleep.

"At midnight the cry rang out: 'Here's the bridegroom! Come out to meet him!'

"Then all the virgins woke up and trimmed their lamps. The foolish ones said to the wise, 'Give us some of your oil; our lamps are going out.'

"'No,' they replied, 'there may not be enough for both us and you. Instead, go to those who sell oil and buy some for yourselves.'

"But while they were on their way to buy the oil, the bridegroom arrived. The virgins who were ready went in with him to the wedding banquet. And the door was shut.

"Later the others also came. 'Lord, Lord,' they said, 'open the door for us!'

"But he replied, 'Truly I tell you, I don't know you.'

"Therefore keep watch, because you do not know the day or the hour (Matt. 25:1-13).

Do you have a vision for your future? For your family? Are you planning for emergencies? We live in perilous times. It is wise to have enough money set aside at home to support yourself for several months, along with a supply of nonperishable food. Have you discussed with your family what to do if all communication were to break down and an emergency were to occur at school, around town, or at work? Are you prepared for the arrival of the Bridegroom?

That day in Cana, when Mary said that they ran out of wine, Jesus responded:

⁴ *"Woman, why do you involve me?" Jesus replied. "My hour has not yet come."*

To walk like Jesus is to know your boundaries

Jesus had a very clear understanding of his mission, and knew that providing wine was not part of it. Family can be the hardest place to keep our boundaries, but as we will see in a moment, those boundaries don't need to be rigid.

Ecclesiastes 3:1–8 says that there is a time for everything, and part of a boundary is the sense of God's timing. Jesus waited for his Father's timing to start his ministry. This would be an ideal opportunity to impress his mother, relatives, and friends—but it would also be dangerous for Jesus to draw attention to himself too early. There are many instances of him fleeing to the mountains or the sea to avoid publicity.

We have spoken of the importance of planning. Your mother, wife, or family may have plans for you, and you may have your own plans. But are they the Lord's plans? We must seek the Lord and submit our plans to him. It may be hard to resist the pressure of your mother or other loved one, but Jesus is your Lord, and he is in charge. There are times when the plans are good, but it's not the Lord's timing. You may be on "hold" right now, waiting for the right time to move ahead with the plans God has for you. Be careful not to push forward with your plans when God seems to have closed the door; you can get into a lot of trouble.

One thing we know is the Lord's time: Salvation. The Bible says, *"Today is the day of salvation"* (2 Cor. 6:2). There are many excuses: You want to experience more of the world, get your life in order before accepting Christ, or not be a hypocrite. Don't wait. You don't know what could happen tomorrow. Today is the day of salvation.

⁵ His mother said to the servants, "Do whatever he tells you."

Mary had also learned that it pays to do what Jesus tells you to do. We noted in verse 4 that Jesus was not happy to be pressured by his mother to solve a problem that was not his to solve. Like many mothers, Mary didn't just accept that and leave things alone. She obligated Jesus to do something by talking to the servants and telling them to do whatever Jesus told them to do. If Jesus did nothing, he would look bad, and he would make his mother look bad.

To walk like Jesus means honoring our parents

It might seem that Jesus didn't honor his parents when he was twelve and stayed behind in Jerusalem to listen to the teachers of the law (Lk. 2:41–52). But now, instead of arguing with Mary or obstinately refusing to do anything, he honored his mother.

The importance of perseverance

You have to admire Mary's persistence. Do you have the faith to persevere? Mary knew that Jesus' word carried great authority; she had witnessed it many times at home. She knew that when Jesus said to do something, you need to do it. Mary had the faith to tell Jesus the problem, hear his response, and put that word into practice. Without the servants' obedience, Jesus' presence and his word would not have meant much. Just like the wise man who built his house on the rock (Matt. 7:24–27), we must obey and put God's word into practice.

⁶ Nearby stood six stone water jars, the kind used by the Jews for ceremonial washing, each holding from twenty to thirty gallons. ⁷ Jesus said to the servants, "Fill the jars with water"; so they filled them to the brim.

When you walk like Jesus, look for empty jars that the Lord can use

Jesus was going to do a miracle, but he needed something to do it. He didn't create wine out of thin air or supply bottles of wine — he uses what we have. These jars could hold between twenty and twenty-six gallons (75–100 liters). In 2017, archaeologists discovered jars like these in Cana. The jars were already there, and they were empty. I could hear someone protest: "But they are for purification rituals! They are for water! We can't use them for wine!" We must trust in Jesus and give him what we have. It may not seem like much, but Jesus needs it. Place it on the altar and make your possessions and talents available to Jesus; then he can do his miracles. Christ can multiply what little you have, just like he multiplied a few fish and loaves of bread to feed multitudes (Mrk. 6:30–44).

It was a simple command, but it was a test of their obedience. Will they do what the carpenter's son tells them to do? Or will they say: "This is nonsense. Why should we fill these jars with water? The problem is with the wine! This is crazy!" But they were servants, just like we are, and their job was to obey. Jesus just said to fill them. If the servants were lazy and didn't want to deal with heavy jars, they could have filled them halfway, but they filled them to the brim. You can impact the size of your miracle. If the Lord asks you to fill the jars, fill them to the brim. When you do something for the Lord, do it to the max. Use all your talents and all your strength.

8 Then he told them, "Now draw some out and take it to the master of the banquet." They did so.

Take of the abundance God gave you and share it with others

Some people's jars are full, but they never take anything out of them! God doesn't do miracles just for show, but to benefit others! They have to take that wine to the one in charge to taste it! There are Christians who attend church every Sunday and leave feeling full. They receive their miracle and spiritual food, but never experience his wonders, because they don't take anything from all that he has given them to share with others.

Once again, we see the need for obedience. It appears that the water became wine when the master of the banquet tasted it. The servants brought him water, despite the possibility of being yelled at for not getting wine. But they did it in obedience to Jesus, and as they went, Jesus performed the miracle.

Are there any empty jars Jesus has given you? It may be that you are not experiencing a miracle because you haven't taken the next step of faith. Maybe you don't know what to say, or you are waiting for a special anointing, but when you obey his word, God will work his miracle. Take from what Jesus has done in your life, bring it to others, and you will see miracles.

9 And the master of the banquet tasted the water that had been turned into wine. He did not realize where it had come from, though the servants who had drawn the water knew. Then he called the bridegroom aside 10 and said, "Everyone brings out the choice wine first and then the cheaper wine after the guests have had too much to drink; but you have saved the best till now."

To walk like Jesus, do everything with excellence

It wasn't Jesus' idea to change water into wine. He wasn't told to do it by his Father. It may seem like it wasn't very important, especially if you believe that it is sinful to drink wine. But everything Jesus did, he did with excellence. When we walk as Jesus did, we offer our best, not only in the church and to God, but also at work and at home.

Have you tasted the new wine?

Imagine the bridegroom's surprise! Not only was his problem solved, but he was also given the best wine this world has ever tasted! Have you tasted Jesus' love and power? He wants to give you the best, and in abundance. He doesn't want to destroy your life; he came to *give* you life. He didn't want to see a wedding ruined because the wine ran out. You may feel like the wine is finished in your life. You may feel hopeless, like the best days of your life are over, but it's not so. We make plans according to our best judgment, and often we fail. We try every way possible to provide the needed wine, but we just don't have the resources, and finally, our only option is to cry out to Jesus. He takes the empty jars of your life and fills them, and fills your heart with his love, joy, and power. He gives us the best because he has saved the best for last.

[11] *What Jesus did here in Cana of Galilee was the first of the signs through which he revealed his glory; and his disciples believed in him.*

Have you seen Jesus' glory? His power and love? When you see his greatness, you have to respond to him! His disciples believed in him. This miracle strengthened their faith, and Jesus wants to strengthen your faith as well. Jesus wants to fill your empty jars and restore your hope. And he wants to walk with you, so you can walk as he walked.

6

Pray as Jesus Taught Us: The Lord's Prayer

Matthew 6:9-13

Now that you are born again and have decided to walk as Jesus walked, it's important to stay in contact with him, talking to him and listening to his voice. How do you feel about your prayer life? Most Christians agree it is important, but also confess that they're not satisfied with it.

It's interesting that just before this prayer, Jesus warned about the danger of "vain repetition," and encouraged us to pray simple prayers from the heart. At first, it might seem that this "formula" prayer goes against that. Especially if, as some do, it is repeated many times at once.

When I was around three years old, my mother taught me a very simple prayer to recite each night as I went to bed. Several years later, she taught me this prayer. I felt so grown up! I had "graduated," and now I could pray the Lord's Prayer! For many years, I recited it every night. It is the best-known prayer in the world. You may have learned it as a child and recited it many times, but do you really know what it means?

9 "This, then, is how you should pray:

"'Our Father

How wonderful to start the day knowing we have a loving Father. My father died in 1978. He was a good man, a Christian, but very reserved. I feel like I never knew him. For years, I longed for his approval, advice, and fatherly embrace. I experienced the "father hunger" that many men feel. Yet I was blessed to have a father in my home; I have heard so many stories of abusive, addicted, and absent fathers. Many don't even know who their father is.

Well, you have a Father who loves you so much that he sent his only Son to die for you. He wants to embrace you. He has adopted you as his son or daughter. We come to Almighty God as a beloved child with our Abba Father. Jesus spoke of that relationship in the verses just preceding this prayer:

But when you pray, go into your room, close the door and pray to your Father, who is unseen. Then your Father, who sees what is done in secret, will reward you. Do not be like the pagans, for your Father knows what you need before you ask him (Matt. 6:6, 8).

In Luke's version of the prayer, Jesus goes on to speak of the Father:

"Which of you fathers, if your son asks for a fish, will give him a snake instead? Or if he asks for an egg, will give him a scorpion? If you then, though you are evil, know how to give good gifts to your children, how much more will your Father in heaven give the Holy Spirit to those who ask him!" (Lk. 11:11–13).

This father/son relationship forms the foundation of every prayer. If you are not reconciled with your heavenly Father, if you are not saved and adopted as his child, before you pray, you need to accept his Son Jesus and give your life to God.

Prayer reflects that intimate relationship with your Father, yet he is also *our* Father. He has a big family! But he always makes time to attend to each of his children. He may not be physically present, but we do have many brothers and sisters to support us in life's trials. You should never feel lonely!

I have one older sister, and I thank God for her, but I always wanted a brother. I wanted lots of children, but I only have one son. Yet now I am part of a big family. And, for many, that family is closer than their earthly family. Even Jesus expressed that:

Someone told him, "Your mother and brothers are standing outside, wanting to speak to you." He replied to him, "Who is my mother, and who are my brothers?" Pointing to his disciples, he said, "Here are my mother and my brothers. For whoever does the will of my Father in heaven is my brother and sister and mother" (Matt. 12:47–50).

In heaven

Many children admire their fathers, seeing them almost as gods. It makes no difference to them if he has a humble job and the family is poor. By the time he reaches adolescence, however, he understands that a wealthy, influential father can be of great help to him. Imagine if your dad were the president! Well, your Father is in heaven and is all-powerful, sovereign, good, and loving.

Jesus and his Father are preparing a place for you right now. The party begins with the wedding supper of the Lamb, after which you will receive your crown and your assignment in his kingdom.

Hallowed be your name

We don't use the word "hallowed" very much; the New Living Translation says, "may your Name be kept holy." God doesn't need to "hallow" his name; that is our responsibility, and we desire that everyone around us would honor it. We know that in the Bible, a name is much more than "God" or "Jesus;" it represents everything that person is, all his attributes. We long to see our Father glorified and lifted up. We will do everything possible to bring him honor and, by our words and actions, encourage others to give him the honor he deserves.

This reflects our obedience to the third of the Ten Commandments:

You shall not use or repeat the name of the Lord your God in vain [that is, lightly or frivolously, in false affirmations or profanely]; for the Lord will not hold him guiltless who takes His name in vain (Ex. 20:7, Amplified Bible).

[10] *Your kingdom come*

God's Kingdom was one of Jesus' favorite topics. To ask that the Kingdom would come recognizes that God already has a kingdom, but it is not yet fully established on earth; it is coming. Meanwhile, we have the responsibility and opportunity to extend it. As Francis Schaeffer said, "There should be substantial healing now in all areas of alienation caused by sin, and total healing at Christ's return." God's Kingdom is present wherever Christ reigns. It starts with you; the Kingdom is within you. Hopefully, it is present in your church or ministry, and it can even be established in a community or workplace.

To say "your kingdom come" acknowledges the tension of being in this world, amid the kingdom of darkness, and recognizing that God has much more in store for us. His Kingdom will be fully established when Christ comes, and this prayer expresses our longing for his return.

Your will be done, on earth as it is in heaven.

An important part of the Kingdom is the absolute authority of the King. His will is always done in heaven, where there is total obedience and submission to his Lordship.

We might expect a sovereign God to impose his will, but he has given us free will. The answer to this prayer begins with us, and the decisions we make:

Therefore, I urge you, brothers and sisters, in view of God's mercy, to offer your bodies as a living sacrifice, holy and pleasing to God—this is your true and proper worship. Do not conform to the pattern of this world, but be transformed by the renewing of your mind. Then you will be able to test and approve what God's will is—his good, pleasing and perfect will (Rom. 12:1–2).

If we are serious about doing his will, we must study the Scriptures and pray with open hearts to discern what it is. What do you know about his will? Have you thought about what heaven is like? Do you have any idea what God's will is for you and your family?

[11] Give us today our daily bread.

Jesus said, *"Man does not live by bread alone"* (Lk. 4:4, Deut. 8:3), so we know we are asking for more than bread. We acknowledge that everything we need comes from God and express our faith and confidence that he will supply it.

There are four important things to note:

1. Starting here, all the requests are plural. In the West, we tend to be very individualistic, but Middle Eastern culture is more corporate. Perhaps there was a reason we always prayed this prayer as a congregation in the church where I grew up. We are praying here not only for ourselves but

for the whole Body of Christ. When we are saved, we become part of Christ's Body, a community of believers.

2. Jesus just said (v. 8): *Your Father knows what you need before you ask.* So if he already knows, and this is something so basic, why include it in this model prayer? We are expressing our dependence on our Father for everything in life.

3. We are asking for bread—for what we need, and no more.

4. It is our *daily* bread. We need to live one day at a time. We go to God every day for that bread, just like Israel went out every morning to collect the manna. In the same chapter, Jesus warns about worrying over the future, and the need to trust God day by day:

[25] *"Therefore I tell you, do not worry about your life, what you will eat or drink; or about your body, what you will wear. Is not life more than food, and the body more than clothes?* [26] *Look at the birds of the air; they do not sow or reap or store away in barns, and yet your heavenly Father feeds them. Are you not much more valuable than they?* [27] *Can any one of you by worrying add a single hour to your life?*

[28] *"And why do you worry about clothes? See how the flowers of the field grow. They do not labor or spin.* [29] *Yet I tell you that not even Solomon in all his splendor was dressed like one of these.* [30] *If that is how God clothes the grass of the field, which is here today and tomorrow is thrown into the fire, will he not much more clothe you—you of little faith?* [31] *So do not worry, saying, 'What shall we eat?' or 'What shall we drink?' or 'What shall we wear?'* [32] *For the pagans run after all these things, and your heavenly Father knows that you need them.* [33] *But seek first his*

kingdom and his righteousness, and all these things will be given to you as well. ³⁴ Therefore do not worry about tomorrow, for tomorrow will worry about itself. Each day has enough trouble of its own.

That short phrase, *"give us today our daily bread,"* covers everything Jesus says in these verses. We trust God for what we need. Prayer frees us from worry, and faith frees us to be busy seeking God's Kingdom—the same request we just made (*may your Kingdom come*). Our heavenly Father will give us everything we need—we don't have to stress over seeking money and material things.

¹² And forgive us our debts, as we also have forgiven our debtors.

Traditionally, some Christians use the words "debts" and "debtors," while others say "trespasses," and "those who trespass against us." I used to think of that as someone trespassing onto my property, or someone who owed me money. In a sense, we are talking about violating the boundaries God has established. But Jesus isn't thinking of financial debts, or trespassing in that sense; the New Living Translation makes it very clear: *"and forgive us our sins, as we have forgiven those who sin against us."*

Praise God for the assurance of forgiven sin! *If we confess our sins, he is faithful and just and will forgive us our sins and purify us from all unrighteousness* (1 Jn. 1:9). We don't have to earn that forgiveness; it is purely by faith in Jesus' work on the cross. We don't have to say a certain number of "Our Fathers;" it is a gift of God's grace. It is the accuser of the brethren, Satan, who sows doubts about our forgiveness and condemns us, but *"there is now no condemnation for those who are in Christ Jesus"* (Rom. 8:1).

There is a critical condition for receiving that forgiveness: we must forgive those who have sinned against us. It says "as we *have* forgiven." *Before* coming to God in prayer, examine yourself to see if there is someone you need to forgive. This is so important that immediately after the prayer, Jesus comes back to emphasize it:

14 For if you forgive other people when they sin against you, your heavenly Father will also forgive you. 15 But if you do not forgive others their sins, your Father will not forgive your sins.

Jesus clearly says that our forgiveness is conditional: if we don't forgive, God does not forgive us. Unforgiveness is a salvation issue and will block your prayers. God does not ask you to do something impossible; he will give you the grace to forgive.

Jesus also devoted a parable to this topic:

Then Peter came to Jesus and asked, "Lord, how many times shall I forgive my brother or sister who sins against me? Up to seven times?"

Jesus answered, "I tell you, not seven times, but seventy-seven times.

"Therefore, the kingdom of heaven is like a king who wanted to settle accounts with his servants. As he began the settlement, a man who owed him ten thousand bags of gold was brought to him. Since he was not able to pay, the master ordered that he and his wife and his children and all that he had be sold to repay the debt.

"At this the servant fell on his knees before him. 'Be patient with me,' he begged, 'and I will pay back everything.' The servant's master took pity on him, canceled the debt and let him go.

"But when that servant went out, he found one of his fellow servants who owed him a hundred silver coins. He grabbed him and began to choke him. 'Pay back what you owe me!' he demanded.

"His fellow servant fell to his knees and begged him, 'Be patient with me, and I will pay it back.'

"But he refused. Instead, he went off and had the man thrown into prison until he could pay the debt. When the other servants saw what had happened, they were outraged and went and told their master everything that had happened.

"Then the master called the servant in. 'You wicked servant,' he said, 'I canceled all that debt of yours because you begged me to. Shouldn't you have had mercy on your fellow servant just as I had on you?' In anger his master handed him over to the jailers to be tortured, until he should pay back all he owed.

"This is how my heavenly Father will treat each of you unless you forgive your brother or sister from your heart." (Matt. 18:21–35)

Jesus wants to make it as clear as possible: our salvation and forgiveness are conditional. If we don't forgive—from the heart!—we will not be forgiven. It is impossible to pay such a huge debt from prison. The torture Jesus mentions is probably hell. God is our Father, but failure to forgive others after experiencing his great mercy provokes his wrath.

Like Peter, we want to know the limit. For him, to forgive seven times was a lot. We are not going to count seventy-seven times (or seven times seventy, as some translate it). We must continue to forgive and not hold anything against anyone. Why? Because God has forgiven so much. Like the servant who was pardoned, we want to bargain with God. He asked for a chance to repay his debt, but that would be impossible. Our debt to God is so great that it is impossible to repay. It is only through God's mercy that we are justified and forgiven. Thus, we must always be merciful to others.

One of the most common things blocking our prayers is unforgiveness. Is there someone you need to forgive?

¹³ And lead us not into temptation, but deliver us from the evil one.

We started the prayer in our Father's arms, in the glory of his Kingdom. We finish on very practical terms, acknowledging how hard it is to live in this world:

- We have to ask for and work for our daily bread—it is not guaranteed.
- We will sin; we need forgiveness.
- Others are going to sin against us.
- We will be tempted.
- Finally, there is an evil one, a devil, who wants to enslave us.

Would God ever lead us into temptation or tempt us? The New Living Translation probably reflects Jesus' meaning: *And don't let us yield to temptation.* If we believe we can resist temptation in our own strength, or if we think we are so spiritual that we are exempt from temptation, we will surely fall. We will be tempted with vile thoughts, which will make us question our salvation, but we only sin when we fall into the temptation. To avoid falling, we must recognize the temptation; part of this request is asking God to open our eyes to it. Then we can trust that God will give us a way out of it:

So, if you think you are standing firm, be careful that you don't fall! No temptation has overtaken you except what is common to mankind. And God is faithful; he will not let you be tempted beyond what you can bear. But when you are tempted, he will also provide a way out so that you can endure it (1 Cor. 10:12–13; the same verse you hopefully memorized back in Chapter 4!).

The last petition (*deliver us from the evil one*) is a daily prayer for deliverance. We often wait for someone with a deliverance ministry, or may battle for years with bad habits and the enemy's strongholds. However, Jesus recognizes that Satan is always trying to destroy us. God wants to free us from those bondages before they harm us and others. As we pray, we should reflect on how we have been tempted, where we have fallen, and where we need deliverance. Then, in faith, we destroy those strongholds, and in the Name of Jesus, we are freed from the evil one! Yes, Jesus wants to deliver you!

For yours is the kingdom and the power and the glory forever. Amen.

Some manuscripts (not the best) conclude the prayer with these words, which redirect the focus back to God and his glory. We don't want to end the prayer focused on the evil one!

You may have learned this prayer in another translation, but the meaning is the same. For variety, try praying it from various translations. It is great to pray it as written, or to use it as a model for your prayers. You may be afraid of getting into a routine, or "vain repetition," but if you are sincere and are seeking God, there probably is not much danger of that. It was Jesus who said, "This *is how you should pray*" (v. 9), and *"When you pray, say"* (in Luke's version, Lk. 11:2). How about devoting a month to learn more about this prayer and make it part of your life?

7

How to get answers to your prayers

The Lord's Prayer includes worship, confession, petition, and spiritual warfare, yet most Christians view prayer as a means of obtaining what they want from God. Indeed, the Bible encourages us to make our requests known to him. There are many teachings on how to get your prayers answered, but what better teacher than Jesus? He was a man of prayer, and gave us straightforward teaching about it, starting in the Sermon on the Mount, in Matthew 6:

⁵ "And when you pray, do not be like the hypocrites, for they love to pray standing in the synagogues and on the street corners to be seen by others. Truly I tell you, they have received their reward in full.

Pray humbly, not to impress others

There will always be hypocrites. They pray too, but they try to impress others with their spirituality through their long, eloquent prayers. If they are looking for recognition from others, they may receive it, but that is all they will get. God is not impressed.

Jesus told a parable to make his point more straightforward:

73

To some who were confident of their own righteousness and looked down on everyone else, Jesus told this parable: "Two men went up to the temple to pray, one a Pharisee and the other a tax collector. The Pharisee stood by himself and prayed: 'God, I thank you that I am not like other people—robbers, evildoers, adulterers—or even like this tax collector. I fast twice a week and give a tenth of all I get.'

"But the tax collector stood at a distance. He would not even look up to heaven, but beat his breast and said, 'God, have mercy on me, a sinner.'

"I tell you that this man, rather than the other, went home justified before God. For all those who exalt themselves will be humbled, and those who humble themselves will be exalted." (Lk. 18:9–14)

Leaders and long-time believers may be more susceptible to this sin. The problem here is:

- Self-confidence
- Self-righteousness
- Self-exaltation (feeling you are better than everyone else)

The Greek says, *"he was praying this to himself."* God doesn't hear that prayer; he listens to the humble person. Is your humility evident in your prayers? Or do you arrogantly come to God, demanding that he do what you want?

Pray in secret

⁶ But when you pray, go into your room, close the door and pray to your Father, who is unseen. Then your Father, who sees what is done in secret, will reward you.

How great to know that God has heard your prayer. He knows what is going on in your "prayer closet," and certainly will reward every sincere prayer that you offer to him.

There is nothing wrong with praying out loud in church or a prayer meeting, but the foundation of our prayer is an intimate relationship with our Father. Sometimes there is so much noise in church that it is hard to hear God, and we find him in that quiet place. You may need to get up early in the morning to be alone with God, or spend a night in prayer, or leave the house to find a solitary place.

That is the example Jesus gave his disciples:

Very early in the morning, while it was still dark, Jesus got up, left the house and went off to a solitary place, where he prayed (Mrk. 1:35).

One of those days Jesus went out to a mountainside to pray, and spent the night praying to God (Lk. 6:12).

After he had dismissed them, he went up on a mountainside by himself to pray (Matt. 14:23).

But Jesus often withdrew to lonely places and prayed (Lk. 5:16).

Do you have that private place where you can freely talk with your Father?

Be careful of vain repetition

[7] And when you pray, do not keep on babbling like pagans, for they think they will be heard because of their many words. [8] Do not be like them, for your Father knows what you need before you ask him.

This raises two important questions:

1. How many times should we repeat the same prayer?

A lengthy prayer, or simple repetition of a formulaic prayer, does not necessarily move God. Prayer is conversing with God; there is no need for eloquence. He is looking for a sincere heart; a person who honestly offers his worship and thanksgiving, along with his needs.

2. If God knows what you need before you ask him, why pray? Or should you simply thank him, with the faith and confidence that he already knows, and is going to provide what you need? The problem is thinking that prayer obligates God to do what we ask. We can confidently draw close to Abba Father and share our hearts. He wants to hear everything, but, like an earthly father, not just requests for more blessings.

The importance of perseverance

We must balance these two questions with Christ's other teachings. Jesus also encouraged perseverance in prayer:

Then Jesus told his disciples a parable to show them that they should always pray and not give up. He said: "In a certain town there was a judge who neither feared God nor cared what people thought. And there was a widow in that town who kept coming to him with the plea, 'Grant me justice against my adversary.'

"For some time he refused. But finally he said to himself, 'Even though I don't fear God or care what people think, yet because this widow keeps bothering me, I will see that she gets justice, so that she won't eventually come and attack me!'"

And the Lord said, "Listen to what the unjust judge says. And will not God bring about justice for his chosen ones, who cry out to him day and night? Will he keep putting them off? I tell you, he will see that they get justice, and quickly. However, when the Son of Man comes, will he find faith on the earth?" (Lk. 18:1–8)

Jesus' purpose in telling this parable is clear: You should always pray and not give up. This judge had the authority and ability to help a poor widow. To make his point even stronger, Jesus made this judge hard-hearted and godless. Despite that, the widow was *"driving me crazy"* and *"wearing me out."* (NLT) To get rid of her he gave her what she wanted.

If an unrighteous judge responded to her persistence, how much more our loving Father!

- You are his chosen one, his adopted son or daughter, whom he loves.

- Surely God will bring about justice for you.

- He will not keep putting you off, but will act quickly (although it might not seem quick enough for you!).

- You need to cry out to him day and night (but not with "babbling," vain repetitions).

- Despite these promises and what we know about God, few have the faith to persevere and receive from their Father like this widow.

Jesus told another, similar parable:

Then Jesus said to them, "Suppose you have a friend, and you go to him at midnight and say, 'Friend, lend me three loaves of bread; a friend of mine on a journey has come to me, and I have no food to offer him.' And suppose the one inside answers, 'Don't bother me. The door is already locked, and my children and I are in bed. I can't get up and give you anything.' I tell you, even though he will not get up and give you the bread because of friendship, yet because of your shameless audacity he will surely get up and give you as much as you need.

"So I say to you: Ask and it will be given to you; seek and you will find; knock and the door will be opened to you. For everyone who asks receives; the one who seeks finds; and to the one who knocks, the door will be opened.

"Which of you fathers, if your son asks for a fish, will give him a snake instead? Or if he asks for an egg, will give him a scorpion? If you then, though you are evil, know how to give good gifts to your children, how much more will your Father in heaven give the Holy Spirit to those who ask him!" (Lk. 11:5–13)

This time, it is a friend asking his neighbor, but it is late, and the man is in bed (perhaps in an intimate moment with his wife). He doesn't want to be bothered, but because of the neighbor's *"shameless audacity,"* insistence, and persistence, he gives him the bread—again, just to be rid of him. There is a place for shameless audacity in our prayers!

Ask, seek, and knock

These words in Luke are almost the same as Jesus' words in the Sermon on the Mount, Matthew 7:7–11:

"Ask, and it will be given to you; seek, and you will find; knock, and it will be opened to you. For everyone who asks receives, and he who seeks finds, and to him who knocks it will be opened. Or what man is there among you who, when his son asks for a loaf, will give him a stone? Or if he asks for a fish, he will not give him a snake, will he? If you then, being evil, know how to give good gifts to your children, how much more will your Father who is in heaven give what is good to those who ask Him!

There are amazing promises here:

- You need to ask God, and keep on asking. The verb is progressive, meaning not just once, but perhaps until you receive. This is the problem that James pointed out in Chapter 4, verse 2, of his letter: *You do not have because you do not ask God*. But then James explains why, at times, despite the promise, we don't get what we ask for: *When you ask, you do not receive, because you ask with wrong motives, that you may spend what you get on your pleasures* (v. 3). If we have good motives and ask according to God's heart, we will receive what we ask for.

- You must seek God, seek his face, and seek his will. The Jew would automatically think of these promises from Jeremiah: *For I know the plans I have for you," declares the Lord, "plans to prosper you and not to harm you, plans to give you hope and a future. Then you will call on me and come and pray to me, and I will listen to you. You will seek me and find me when you seek me with all your heart* (Jer. 29:11–13). We are very familiar with the first part; we like the promise of prosperity, hope, and a future. But that promise is given in the context of prayer and seeking God with all our heart. We may not find God because we are not seeking him and praying with our whole heart—we seek his blessing instead of *him*.

- When you knock at the door, God will open it for you. But, which door? That may be the issue: we often knock at the wrong door and are disappointed when nobody answers—or someone answers whom we don't want to see. This could be the door of heaven, the door to the most holy place. There is a progression here: first, we ask, then we seek God's face, and finally, we just want to be in his presence. The door could also be a door of service, opportunities God has for you: *See, I have placed before you an open door that no one can shut* (Rev. 3:8).

Then Jesus, perhaps still thinking about the evil judge or the irritated neighbor, compares God to an earthly father. Any father would give his son bread when he asks for it (and certainly not something deadly like a snake); how much more will your heavenly Father give you good things!

Do you have that concept of God? He loves you even more than you love your own son, and wants to bless you and answer your prayers. In Luke, Jesus says God will surely give his Holy Spirit to those who ask. Have you asked to be filled with the Holy Spirit?

Jesus' entire teaching is designed to motivate us to pray more. God is your loving Father. He wants to hear your prayer. He wants to talk with you. He has good things for you. If you have been discouraged with prayer, this is the time to find that secret place and seek God. He is waiting for you there. Think about the widow and the neighbor; day and night come to God, pour out your pain, your longings, and your heart before him. Prayer is so simple, but so powerful and fulfilling!

Ask! It will be given to you. Seek! You will find. Knock! The door will be opened to you.

8

Mountains Cast Into the Sea

W ouldn't it be great to have the faith to cast a mountain into the sea? Or just to get your prayers answered? Jesus says it is possible. In this first passage, he shows us how to do it, and he makes it look so easy!

"Have faith in God," Jesus answered. "Truly I tell you, if anyone says to this mountain, 'Go, throw yourself into the sea,' and does not doubt in their heart but believes that what they say will happen, it will be done for them. Therefore I tell you, whatever you ask for in prayer, believe that you have received it, and it will be yours. And when you stand praying, if you hold anything against anyone, forgive them, so that your Father in heaven may forgive you your sins." (Mrk. 11:22–25)

Matthew gives the same promise (and its context), but omits that last verse about forgiving others:

Early in the morning, as Jesus was on his way back to the city, he was hungry. Seeing a fig tree by the road, he went up to it but found nothing on it except leaves. Then he said to it, "May you never bear fruit again!" Immediately the tree withered.

When the disciples saw this, they were amazed. "How did the fig tree wither so quickly?" they asked.

Jesus replied, "Truly I tell you, if you have faith and do not doubt, not only can you do what was done to the fig tree, but also you can say to this mountain, 'Go, throw yourself into the sea,' and it will be done. If you believe, you will receive whatever you ask for in prayer." (Matt. 21:18–22)

First, some keywords:

- *Have faith.* Faith must be *in God.* When we say something, we must say it *believing.*

- Jesus emphasizes the certainty of what he says: *Truly I tell you.*

- It's not just for giants of the faith; it is for *anyone.*

- When we ask for something, we must *believe that we have already received it.* It is done.

Two things will prevent us from receiving:

- Doubt. It is very common to have doubts; we all fight them. But Jesus says that even the slightest doubt can keep God from answering our prayers.

- Lack of forgiveness. If there is sin we haven't confessed to God (and thus it has not been forgiven), we won't see the miracle. To be forgiven, first we must forgive others. Jesus knows that we may become aware of someone we need to forgive as we stand praying.

Jesus' earthly brother wrote:

If any of you lacks wisdom, you should ask God, who gives generously to all without finding fault, and it will be given to you. But when you ask, you must believe and not doubt, because the one who doubts is like a wave of the sea, blown and tossed by the wind. That person should not expect to receive anything from the Lord. Such a person is double-minded and unstable in all they do (Jas. 1:5–8).

- Once again, this applies to all, to everyone, because God gives generously. That means you.

- The only requirement is to believe, to ask in faith.

- Doubt is very serious. The person who doubts *will not receive anything from the Lord*.

The fig tree seems trivial, but if we learn to walk in that faith, we can walk in that power. With faith, we can speak something (even as frivolous as casting a mountain into the ocean!) and see it happen.

What doubts do you have? Confess them to the Lord and ask his help to overcome them. Your faith doesn't depend on your feelings, but on the truth of God's Word. Study the Bible, apologetics (the reasons for your faith), and other Christians' testimonies. Avoid literature, internet sites, or friends that undermine your faith. Be active in your church—the worship, preaching of the Word, and God's presence will help silence your doubts.

Are you double-minded and unstable in everything you do? There may be a deeper problem than just doubts about your faith. Examine yourself to try to find where that comes from, and get help if necessary. Jesus wants you firm in your faith, not blown and tossed about by the wind.

Three keys for answered prayer from the Upper Room

It could appear that Jesus was not very careful in his choice of words—there are several "blank checks" regarding prayer, including words like "whatever." For example, he gives four promises for answered prayer in the Upper Room discourse:

*And I will do **whatever** you ask in my name, so that the Father may be glorified in the Son. You may ask me for anything in my name, and I will do it* (Jn. 14:13–14).

*If you remain in me and my words remain in you, ask **whatever** you wish, and it will be done for you* (Jn. 15:7).

*You did not choose me, but I chose you and appointed you so that you might go and bear fruit—fruit that will last—and so that **whatever** you ask in my name the Father will give you* (Jn. 15:16).

*In that day you will no longer ask me anything. Very truly I tell you, my Father will give you **whatever** you ask in my name. Until now you have not asked for anything in my name. Ask and you will receive, and your joy will be complete* (Jn. 16:23–24).

Once again, Jesus uses impressive words:

- It is "*whatever*" you ask the Father; he will give it to you.

- Jesus uses words like "*very truly*" to add even more force to the promises.

- God is glorified when he answers our prayers (and he wants to glorify himself!).

- Answered prayer helps fulfill our call to be fruitful. When our request involves that fruit, we can be sure that God will answer it.

- We experience Jesus' complete joy when God answers our prayers.

- In these examples, prayer involves requests. It is okay to ask God for something!

With all that encouragement, why don't we see more answered prayers?

- We must ask "in his name," as if it were Jesus himself making the request. Our hearts must be in sync with his. Maybe John recalled that night in the Upper Room when he wrote: *This is the confidence we have in approaching God: that if we ask anything according to his will, he hears us* (1 John 5:14). The request must be "according to his will."

- We must remain (abide) in Jesus, and his words remain in us. If we don't nurture our relationship with Jesus and walk in accordance with his Word, we will struggle in our spiritual life and lack that close fellowship with Christ.

- The third key comes from James 4:2–3: *You do not have because you do not ask God. When you ask, you do not receive, because you ask with wrong motives, that you may spend what you get on your pleasures.* Sometimes we simply fail to ask. We hardly spend any time in prayer. More frequently, we ask selfishly, with wrong motives, focused on our desires and pleasure.

An example of Jesus in prayer

This is Jesus' last recorded prayer:

Then Jesus went with his disciples to a place called Gethsemane, and he said to them, "Sit here while I go over there and pray." He took Peter and the two sons of Zebedee along with him, and he began to be sorrowful and troubled. Then he said to them, "My soul is overwhelmed with sorrow to the point of death. Stay here and keep watch with me."

Going a little farther, he fell with his face to the ground and prayed, "My Father, if it is possible, may this cup be taken from me. Yet not as I will, but as you will."

Then he returned to his disciples and found them sleeping. "Couldn't you men keep watch with me for one hour?" he asked Peter. "Watch and pray so that you will not fall into temptation. The spirit is willing, but the flesh is weak."

He went away a second time and prayed, "My Father, if it is not possible for this cup to be taken away unless I drink it, may your will be done."

When he came back, he again found them sleeping, because their eyes were heavy. So he left them and went away once more and prayed the third time, saying the same thing.

Then he returned to the disciples and said to them, "Are you still sleeping and resting? Look, the hour has come, and the Son of Man is delivered into the hands of sinners. Rise! Let us go! Here comes my betrayer!" (Matt. 26:36–46)

In times of anguish, we need the presence and support of brothers and sisters in Christ. Unfortunately, the three disciples closest to Jesus couldn't comply with his simple request; they couldn't keep watch with him for one hour. They fell asleep. And we are no better; we sleep, rest, and take it easy when we most need to be watching out for the devil. In the Lord's Prayer, we ask: "lead us not into temptation." Here, Jesus says we must watch and pray so we don't fall into that temptation. Sadly, for too many of us, the spirit may be willing, but our flesh is weak.

Some teach that we should never say "if it is your will" in our prayers. They say it betrays a lack of faith; we should simply declare what we want God to do. We almost end up demanding that God do our will! But that goes against the submission expressed in the Lord's Prayer (*Your will be done on earth as it is in heaven*), and also in Jesus' prayer here. Jesus asked to avoid the cross *"if it is possible,"* but submitted himself to the Father's will: *"Yet not as I will, but as you will."* Jesus was fighting for his life; three times, he asked the same thing. Perhaps the author of Hebrews was referring to this prayer when he wrote:

During the days of Jesus' life on earth, he offered up prayers and petitions with fervent cries and tears to the one who could save him from death, and he was heard because of his reverent submission (Heb. 5:7).

It says he was heard—but he didn't get what he asked for. Despite all the promises of receiving what we ask, ultimately, we must submit to God's will. Shouldn't that be easy? Don't you believe he knows best? Every good gift comes from God! Trust him!

Pray!

We have repeatedly seen that God wants to communicate with us and answer our prayers, and has given us many precious promises to encourage us to pray. Many books have been written about prayer. It is a deep topic, but it is not complicated or difficult. Just do it!

9

Pray Like Jesus Prayed, Just Before His Death

John 17

Prepare to enter holy ground, as we see Jesus' heart in his longest recorded prayer. It is not his last prayer before the cross (which we looked at in the previous chapter), but Jesus knew that within hours he would be betrayed, arrested, and crucified. A man's prayer when he faces death reveals his faith and his heart.

JESUS' DESIRE TO GLORIFY HIS FATHER

¹After Jesus said this, he looked toward heaven and prayed: "Father, the hour has come. Glorify your Son, that your Son may glorify you.

We know God doesn't dwell on some cloud or distant planet; he dwells outside our concept of space. But we lift our hands in worship, Jesus ascended to heaven, and here he looked toward heaven as he prayed. Instinctively, we know that God dwells in a high place, above us.

Father

Jesus opens the prayer just as he taught us in the Lord's Prayer. God is your Father. He adopted you as his child, and you can rest secure in his arms. Run to your Father with complete confidence and boldness!

The hour has come

God has plans—for each of us, and all history. The Father had a plan for Jesus, who was fully aware of his destiny. Jesus had to wait for the right time, and now it had come. It may be that the time has come for you to be released into a new ministry, or for a fresh revelation of God's plan for your life. Do you know your destiny? The purpose of your life? The time will also come for each of us to die. Will you be ready for that hour, or the hour when Jesus returns?

Father and Son glorify each other

Jesus' first request is to be glorified. He will be glorified the next day in the agony of the cross, and even more in the victory of his resurrection. But Jesus isn't trying to exalt himself; he wants to be glorified *so that* he can glorify his Father. The Father and Son try to outdo each other in glorifying one another. The Father loves to glorify Jesus, and Jesus longs to glorify the Father.

What does it mean to glorify? The dictionary says: to make glorious by bestowing honor, praise, or admiration; to recognize who someone is and give them glory, demonstrating their approval and interest in that person.

The amazing thing is that God also glorifies us! He sanctifies us, cleanses us, gives us a glorified body, and even allows us to share in his glory. Just as Jesus glorified his Father throughout his life, our goal should be to glorify God in everything we do. Do you long to glorify God? How can you bring glory to Jesus today?

² For you granted him authority over all people that he might give eternal life to all those you have given him.

Jesus glorified his Father by wisely using the power given him, bringing salvation to those the Father had given him. To glorify implies giving, and, in the Greek, the verb "give" appears three times in this verse, and 19 times in this chapter! It is the keyword of this prayer.

Three things given

First, the Father gave Jesus authority, or power, over all people. That means your family, your boss, and the leaders of your nation. That authority is given; it cannot be earned. How great to know that in this crazy world, Jesus is sovereign and has authority over everyone. The Father can give you power and authority as well—in your family, church, job, or ministry.

Power and authority are tricky. Of course, Jesus handled them perfectly, but power corrupts, and it is easy for authority to go to someone's head. God doesn't give us power and authority to make us haughty and overbearing, but to benefit those he wants to bless. The Father granted Jesus authority *so that* he could give us eternal life, our salvation (the second gift in this verse). We can't earn salvation through our good works; it is a gift that Christ purchased with his blood and gives to those who receive him as Lord and Savior.

The third thing given is an unknown number of men and women whom the Father gave to Jesus. The idea of election appears various times in this prayer—it is an uncomfortable topic for many, but something we can't avoid in the Scriptures. God's will is that all those he has given to Jesus would receive eternal life.

What is eternal life?

³ Now this is eternal life: that they know you, the only true God, and Jesus Christ, whom you have sent.

We tend to think of eternal life as endless time, but Jesus says here it is not a matter of *quantity*, but of *quality*. Eternal life is a relationship, *knowing* the Father and *knowing* Jesus. God operates outside our concept of time. You can experience eternal life right now!

There are many gods in this world, but we know that the one true God has no name other than those revealed in Scripture. Nor are there many paths to God—Jesus is the only way to the Father. Jesus introduces another important word found several times in this prayer: sent. Jesus was sent to earth by his Father.

Do you have eternal life? Would you say you know the Father? Do you know Jesus? How can you get to know them better and experience more eternal life, right now?

I have finished the work

⁴ I have brought you glory on earth by finishing the work you gave me to do.

When the Father sent Jesus to this earth, he came with a job to do. He spent thirty years preparing for that work, and it took him only three years to finish it. He trained the disciples, revealed who God is through his words and wonders, and was completely obedient, thus bringing glory to his Father.

How great to be able to say, "I have finished the work." Once again, this job was *given* to him. It is not for us to choose our job in the kingdom. We must seek God and wait on him for that work to be revealed; then we are obligated to work with all our heart, and thus bring glory to God.

Do you know what work God has given you to do? How is it going? Are you progressing in it? Perhaps you have finished it and can rest now?

5 And now, Father, glorify me in your presence with the glory I had with you before the world began.

Jesus knows that soon he will suffer the agony of crucifixion, but he can bear it, knowing that he is going back to his Father's side to share again in the glory he voluntarily left to come to this world.

JESUS PRAYS FOR HIS DISCIPLES

6 "I have revealed you to those whom you gave me out of the world. They were yours; you gave them to me and they have obeyed your word.

Jesus said that if you saw him, you had seen the Father (Jn. 14:9). In his daily life, words, and deeds, Jesus perfectly revealed who God is. You can also reveal something of what God is like, so that others can see Jesus in you.

In this second section, Jesus prays for his twelve disciples. They were the focus of his ministry, and they would continue it as they established the church. Jesus loved them. Just as he said, "I have finished the work," now he says, "I have revealed you to them." He can rest, knowing he has done what he was sent to do.

Here we learn more about election: these men *were yours*, they belonged to the Father. The Father chose them for this work, and Jesus spent a night praying to confirm who should be among the twelve (Lk. 6:12). It is a great responsibility to care for and minister to people who are so special to the Father. He gives us a spouse, children, a family, spiritual children, and perhaps a church. We are stewards, charged with caring for them and sharing God's word with them.

Jesus rejoices that they have *obeyed your word*. It is important to receive the word, but even more important to obey it. Jesus is confident that if they obey it, they will manifest his name to the world and finish the work he has given them to do.

Give the word you receive

⁷ Now they know that everything you have given me comes from you. ⁸ For I gave them the words you gave me and they accepted them. They knew with certainty that I came from you, and they believed that you sent me.

At the center of Jesus' work with his disciples was the word: His Father gave him the words, Jesus gave them to the disciples, and they received them. It's a simple yet crucial process. On another occasion, Jesus said that he spoke nothing on his own account, but only the words given to him by the Father (Jn. 5:19; 12:49). God's Word is powerful. How is it, then, that we somehow feel we can preach whatever we feel like preaching? Shouldn't we wait on God for his word, and then give it as we have received it?

As the disciples received the word, three things happened:

- They were convinced that everything Jesus had was received from his Father. How great to live in such a way that others recognize that it is not our talent or intelligence, but that God has given us everything we have.

- They knew with certainty, intellectually, that Jesus came from the Father.

- They believed in their hearts, in faith, that the Father sent him.

As we receive the Spirit-inspired Word, the Spirit confirms it as true. The disciples could see the intimate relationship Jesus had with his Father and accepted that he was God.

All I have is yours

⁹ I pray for them. I am not praying for the world, but for those you have given me, for they are yours.¹⁰ All I have is yours, and all you have is mine. And glory has come to me through them.

Once again, Jesus acknowledges that his disciples were given to him; they belong to the Father. If we adopt that attitude with the people entrusted to us, it could save us from pride and many abuses. We also see an exchange between these two persons of the Trinity: Everything Jesus has belongs to the Father, and the Father holds nothing back from the Son. God does the same with us: As we give everything to him (our money, talents, and possessions—all that we are), he withholds nothing from us.

On other occasions, Jesus prayed for the world, but now his prayer is only for these special men whom his Father had given him. Jesus glorified the Father in his earthly life and was also glorified through his disciples. How? Others saw God's power and character in them, noticed that they had been with Jesus, and glorified God.

Has Jesus been glorified in your life and church? How? If not, is there something you could change so he would be glorified?

That they may be one, as we are one

¹¹ I will remain in the world no longer, but they are still in the world, and I am coming to you. Holy Father, protect them by the power of your name, the name you gave me, so that they may be one as we are one.

Jesus was already missing his beloved disciples. Since he will no longer be with them, he asks his Father to protect them. He knows the devil will come against them and will do everything possible to divide them and create conflicts.

The heaviest burden on Jesus' heart that night was for their unity; not just superficial unity, but the same unity he enjoyed with the Father, the perfect unity of the Godhead. It is a request we see several times in this prayer.

12 While I was with them, I protected them and kept them safe by that name you gave me. None has been lost except the one doomed to destruction so that Scripture would be fulfilled.

Jesus said he finished the work and revealed God's name; now he says he protected them and kept them safe by that name. When he was with them, he did everything necessary to keep them safe. He was always aware that his Father had given them to him. In the same way, we must do everything possible to protect and maintain the unity of those God has given us. But even Jesus faced failure with his disciples; to fulfill the Scriptures, one was doomed to destruction and betrayed him (Judas, a wolf in sheep's clothing). We, too, may experience the pain of losing someone we have discipled.

How good to know that God will protect us, our families, and the people he has entrusted to us, even if there is a Judas who chooses to follow a different path and lose that protection.

The full measure of Jesus' joy

¹³ *"I am coming to you now, but I say these things while I am still in the world, so that they may have the full measure of my joy within them.*

I can imagine that being in Jesus' presence was pure joy, but he knows he is going to the Father, and he doesn't want his disciples to lose that joy. Indeed, he wants them to have the *full measure* of that joy. Jesus has given us his word, so that we may have his joy. That has nothing to do with circumstances, but with the relationship we have with Jesus and the manifestation of what is also a fruit of the Spirit.

Do you have Jesus' joy? In full measure? What is robbing you of that joy?

The world hates us

¹⁴ *I have given them your word and the world has hated them, for they are not of the world any more than I am of the world.*

Here is the fourth thing Jesus did: He gave them God's word.

Now that we are in Christ, we are no longer of this world. In fact, the world hates us. We are in a different kingdom, and the world cannot understand kingdom values; they are under the control of the evil one. Unfortunately, many Christians long for the world's approval, but there is a problem if the world loves us. If we are faithful to Christ and keep his word, the world will hate us.

What we should do, which Jesus did, is give them God's word. Indeed, it is not us that they hate, but the One who gave us his word and sent us to reveal his Name.

Learning to Walk

[15] My prayer is not that you take them out of the world but that you protect them from the evil one. [16] They are not of the world, even as I am not of it.

The solution is not to take us out of the world, although through the centuries many Christians have tried to do that, and live separate from "sinners." It would be great if God snatched us up to heaven the minute we accept Jesus! I am sure every prisoner would come to Christ! But God has a purpose for us here, and he shapes and sanctifies us in the trials of this life.

Jesus repeats that he is not of this world; we are not *of* the world, but we are *in* the world. Jesus' prayer is that the Father would protect us from the evil one. We may be tempted and surrounded by sin, but God will protect us.

[17] Sanctify them by the truth; your word is truth.

Part of that process is our sanctification. God separates us from the world and establishes a new community, cleansing and freeing us from sin. Once again, his word, the sword of the Spirit, is the primary instrument. Are you allowing the word to sanctify you?

God sends us into the world

[18] As you sent me into the world, I have sent them into the world.

In the same way that the Father sent Jesus into the world, now Christ sends us into the world, to experience all that he did in his thirty-three years on earth. Yes, it is true that we are not of the world, and spiritually, God separates us from it. But then, as a soldier sent to war after thorough training, with arms and armor, Jesus sends us into the world with his word to reveal his Name in signs, wonders, and good works.

Jesus left everything and humbled himself to be born as a baby, experiencing what it is like to be a man. We must follow his example of incarnation and enter the world, loving it despite its hatred and rejection of us.

¹⁹ For them I sanctify myself, that they too may be truly sanctified.

Surely it would seem that Jesus was already sanctified, but he is setting himself apart and offering the utmost sacrifice so that we can be sanctified and demonstrate his Name to the world. Jesus did everything for them, and us!

JESUS PRAYS FOR YOU

²⁰ "My prayer is not for them alone. I pray also for those who will believe in me through their message,

Jesus is your high priest! He is praying for you right now! How do we come to believe in Jesus? Through the Word! Somebody shared God's Word with you; do you know someone who needs the Word so they can believe in Jesus?

That the world may believe

²¹ that all of them may be one, Father, just as you are in me and I am in you. May they also be in us so that the world may believe that you have sent me.

Jesus said we are not of the world; the world will hate us. He was not praying for the world, but he still wants the world to believe that the Father sent him. He just said that we believe when we receive the word. But along with the word, the world needs a demonstration of God's love and power. It needs the testimony of a united church.

Unity is Jesus' first petition for the church, and it is not just superficial; it is total union with God: Just as the Father is in Jesus, and just as Jesus is in the Father, we are one in Jesus and the Father.

Our unity flows from our union with God. It is the same intimacy that Jesus had with his Father. If we lack unity, something is probably missing in our union with God. Unfortunately, it seems hard to find this kind of unity. No wonder the church is a joke to the world, and they don't believe in Jesus.

²² I have given them the glory that you gave me, that they may be one as we are one—

This unity is so essential to Jesus that he has given us the same glory the Father gave him. His hope is that with that glory manifest, we would be one. Again, if we lack unity, we probably have not experienced the glory Jesus longs to give us.

Are you aware of the glory Jesus has given the church? Have you seen it? Are you doing your part to promote the unity of the church?

²³ I in them and you in me—so that they may be brought to complete unity. Then the world will know that you sent me and have loved them even as you have loved me.

The Father has loved us with the same love he has for Jesus. The Christian should experience an amazing love that is obvious to the world. When we are filled with that love, we can't help but love our brothers and sisters. Too often, we lack that love.

Our unity also reflects God's love in us. Where there is a problem with unity, there is probably a problem with our experience of God's love. This time Jesus prays for complete, or perfect, unity. This is supernatural. It also presents us with a dilemma: how can we reconcile this?

- On one hand, we have seen tremendous promises for answered prayer, the importance of faith, and praying in God's will. If anyone should have his prayer answered, it would be Jesus, the Son of God! He certainly had no doubts; he knew God's will, and he sought God's glory.

- On the other hand, we see the reality: we have seldom experienced this perfect, complete unity. The world continues in its unbelief, and God is not glorified.

It offers me some encouragement to know that even Jesus didn't have all his prayers answered. The only solution I can suggest to this dilemma is our free will and the pervasiveness of evil and sin in this world, which makes us long even more to be with Jesus in his kingdom.

That they may be with me and see my glory

24 "Father, I want those you have given me to be with me where I am, and to see my glory, the glory you have given me because you loved me before the creation of the world.

Yes, God has a purpose for us in the world, but Jesus wants us with him in heaven! He is preparing a place for us right now. Does it excite you to think about being with Jesus and seeing his glory?

God's love in us, and Christ in us

25 "Righteous Father, though the world does not know you, I know you, and they know that you have sent me. 26 I have made you known to them, and will continue to make you known in order that the love you have for me may be in them and that I myself may be in them."

The revelation of God's Name is an ongoing process that includes studying the Bible. The more we know God, the more we will be filled with his love—not only his love in us, but Jesus himself in us. They are just a few words at the end of the prayer, but, amazingly, Jesus himself lives in us!

What is God's word for you?

This prayer is an intimate communication between Jesus and his Father, but also a challenge to us on various levels:

- Do you know God's plan for your life? What work does he have for you? Are you working in that job?

- Do you have Jesus' joy?

- Are you experiencing perfect unity with brothers and sisters in Christ?

- Are you demonstrating Jesus' Name to the world in word and deed? Do you live with the knowledge that Jesus has sent you into the world?

- Do you care for the people God has entrusted to you, with the understanding that you are a steward, that they belong to God, and that he has given them to you?

- Do you know this same love that the Father has for Jesus?

- Do you walk daily with the understanding that Jesus lives in you?

- Are you glorifying God?

10

Fasting as Jesus Did

We have studied Jesus' teaching on prayer; fasting is another way of communicating with God and making our requests known. Fasting is beneficial and biblical, but the New Testament has very little to say about it.

Jesus' only teaching on fasting

Right after his teaching on prayer in the Sermon on the Mount (Matthew 6), Jesus said:

[16] "When you fast, do not look somber as the hypocrites do, for they disfigure their faces to show others they are fasting. Truly I tell you, they have received their reward in full. [17] But when you fast, put oil on your head and wash your face, [18] so that it will not be obvious to others that you are fasting, but only to your Father, who is unseen; and your Father, who sees what is done in secret, will reward you.

What do we learn about fasting?

- Jesus says "when," not "if." He expected that fasting would be part of the believer's life.

- Like prayer, fasting is private. There are congregational fasts, and we may need to inform family members that we are fasting; however, we generally continue with our

103

regular routine. Jesus expects us to be with other people, although sometimes we may take a retreat for an intense time of prayer and fasting.

- If we fast to impress others with our spirituality, that will be our reward. God is not impressed.

- The Father promises to reward us. The wording is the same as Jesus' statement about prayer.

The experience of Jesus and the disciples

Jesus' only recorded fast was during his forty days of temptation in the wilderness:

After fasting forty days and forty nights, he was hungry (Matthew 4:2).

Fasting prepared and strengthened Jesus for the intense testing and temptation by Satan. The forty days followed the example of great men of the Old Testament, especially the "champion" of fasting, Moses, who probably fasted more than anyone, and with good reason: he had an extremely difficult task.

Religious leaders criticized Jesus and his disciples for not fasting:

They said to him, "John's disciples often fast and pray, and so do the disciples of the Pharisees, but yours go on eating and drinking."

Jesus answered, "Can you make the friends of the bridegroom fast while he is with them? But the time will come when the bridegroom will be taken from them; in those days they will fast" (Lk. 5:33–35).

This part is clear:

- Two very different groups are mentioned: John the Baptist's disciples, and the Pharisees. Both were viewed as being very spiritual, and both fasted, as was common for religious people. Jesus may well have included the Pharisees among the hypocrites he condemned in Matthew 6, but we can assume that John's disciples were sincere.

- It is not the first time Jesus was questioned about his "partying;" his disciples had the same reputation of eating, drinking, and enjoying life.

- Jesus does not defend his disciples or feel the need to justify their lifestyle. We don't know if his audience understood that he was the bridegroom, or how he would be taken away from them. Although many Jews did not accept him as the Messiah, it makes sense that the disciples would rejoice while their Bridegroom was with them.

- As we wait for his return, fasting should be part of our lives.

Now Jesus uses three common-sense examples to communicate the same idea:

He told them this parable: "No one tears a piece out of a new garment to patch an old one. Otherwise, they will have torn the new garment, and the patch from the new will not match the old. And no one pours new wine into old wineskins. Otherwise, the new wine will burst the skins; the wine will run out and the wineskins will be ruined. No, new wine must be poured into new wineskins. And no one after drinking old wine wants the new, for they say, 'The old is better.'" (Lk. 5:36–39)

Almost identical passages are found in Matthew 9:14–17 and Mark 2:18–22. The parable relates to fasting, but how?

- An old garment needs repair. The person also has a new garment, but the two are not compatible; to tear a piece out of the new garment would ruin it, and it wouldn't match the old garment. It is better to discard the old clothes and stick with the new ones.

- New wine is not compatible with old wineskins. If you try to fill the old wineskin, it will burst and be ruined, and the new wine will be lost. The old wineskin has served its purpose; it's best to throw it out and use a new wineskin.

- The third example seems to contradict what Jesus just said. The first two encourage us to forget about the old and go with the new. But with wine, old is better. It seems that Jesus' message is to not look back; don't get nostalgic and return to the old ways. It may seem better, but sooner or later, you have to go with the new wine.

In the context of fasting, then, Jesus seems to be saying that the norms and practices of the Old Covenant don't necessarily apply in his kingdom. To try to carry them over or modify them for the New Covenant won't work. He is making everything new. Yes, his disciples are going to fast, but it may not look like fasting did under the Law.

The only other time Jesus mentioned fasting was in the case of the demonized boy whom the disciples could not help (Matt. 17:14–20 and Mk. 9:14–29). Jesus told his disciples that prayer *and* fasting were necessary to cast out that demon, implying that fasting enhances our spiritual authority.

Two fasts recorded in Acts

While they were worshiping the Lord and fasting, the Holy Spirit said, "Set apart for me Barnabas and Saul for the work to which I have called them." So after they had fasted and prayed, they placed their hands on them and sent them off (Acts 13:2–3).

Fasting gave them increased sensitivity and authority for this special task of hearing from God, setting missionaries apart, and sending them out. Paul and Barnabas learned from this experience, since they were fasting when they installed leaders in a new church:

Paul and Barnabas appointed elders for them in each church and, with prayer and fasting, committed them to the Lord, in whom they had put their trust (Acts 14:23).

Fasting in the Old Testament

The Hebrew word translated "fast" literally means "to cover the mouth." Fasting is also referred to with a word which means "to afflict the soul." It is a way of humbling yourself and denying yourself. In keeping with that, the Lord includes fasting with weeping and mourning as a sign of true repentance:

"Even now," declares the Lord,
  "return to me with all your heart,
  with fasting and weeping and mourning" (Joel 2:12).

The only fast required by the Law was for the Day of Atonement (Lev. 23:27–29)—the person who chose not to fast faced the death penalty. At various times, a king would call a national fast, and there were fasts for special times of repentance and seeking God. David fasted for his son's healing (2 Sam. 12:16). For a time of waiting on God, Daniel prayed and fasted, as he humbled himself with sackcloth and ashes: *So I turned to the Lord God and pleaded with him in prayer and petition, in fasting, and in sackcloth and ashes* (Dan. 9:3).

Jesus' teaching in the Sermon on the Mount was not new; the Old Testament made very clear that an effective fast required a heart that was right with God:

Stop bringing me your meaningless gifts;
  the incense of your offerings disgusts me!
As for your celebrations of the new moon and the Sabbath
  and your special days for fasting—
they are all sinful and false.
  I want no more of your pious meetings (Is. 1:13, NLT).

The most extended and most well-known passage on fasting (Isaiah 58) expands on the same theme:

¹ "Shout it aloud, do not hold back.
  Raise your voice like a trumpet.
Declare to my people their rebellion
  and to the descendants of Jacob their sins.
² For day after day they seek me out;
  they seem eager to know my ways,
as if they were a nation that does what is right
  and has not forsaken the commands of its God.
They ask me for just decisions
  and seem eager for God to come near them.
³ 'Why have we fasted,' they say,
  'and you have not seen it?
Why have we humbled ourselves,
  and you have not noticed?'

Seeking God, learning about his ways, prayer (asking for just decisions), longing to be close to God, and fasting: they are all good, but they do not impress God if your heart is not right. Israel did all of them, and they were perplexed because God did not seem impressed with their fasting. They were blind and in sin and rebellion, having forsaken God's commands. They sound like many Christians today!

"Yet on the day of your fasting, you do as you please
    and exploit all your workers.
⁴ Your fasting ends in quarreling and strife,
    and in striking each other with wicked fists.
You cannot fast as you do today
    and expect your voice to be heard on high.
⁵ Is this the kind of fast I have chosen,
    only a day for people to humble themselves?
Is it only for bowing one's head like a reed
    and for lying in sackcloth and ashes?
Is that what you call a fast,
    a day acceptable to the Lord?

Fasting is good! When we fast properly, our voice will be heard in heaven! But fasting is more than abstaining from food or some other pleasure. It is more than religious asceticism, looking somber, and lying around in sackcloth and ashes. We can fast and still do our own thing! On the same day they were fasting, they were exploiting their workers and fighting.

⁶ "Is not this the kind of fasting I have chosen:
to loose the chains of injustice
    and untie the cords of the yoke,
to set the oppressed free
    and break every yoke?
⁷ Is it not to share your food with the hungry
    and to provide the poor wanderer with shelter—
when you see the naked, to clothe them,
    and not to turn away from your own flesh and blood?

⁸ Then your light will break forth like the dawn,
   and your healing will quickly appear;
then your righteousness will go before you,
   and the glory of the Lord will be your rear guard.
⁹ Then you will call, and the Lord will answer;
   you will cry for help, and he will say: Here am I.

Yes, it is good to seek God and abstain from eating, but he calls us to do right as we fast:

- Break the chains of injustice.
- Untie the cords of the yoke.
- Free the oppressed.
- Break every yoke of bondage.
- Feed the hungry.
- Give shelter to the homeless.
- Clothe the naked.
- Do not turn away from your relatives.

If we fast in that way, God promises that:

- Our light will break forth like the dawn.
- Our healing will be speedy.
- Our righteousness will go before us.
- The glory of the Lord will be our rearguard.
- When we call, God will answer.
- He will say "Here I am" when we cry for help.

"If you do away with the yoke of oppression,
   with the pointing finger and malicious talk,
¹⁰ and if you spend yourselves in behalf of the hungry
   and satisfy the needs of the oppressed,
then your light will rise in the darkness,
   and your night will become like the noonday.
¹¹ The Lord will guide you always;

he will satisfy your needs in a sun-scorched land
and will strengthen your frame.
You will be like a well-watered garden,
like a spring whose waters never fail.
¹² Your people will rebuild the ancient ruins
and will raise up the age-old foundations;
you will be called Repairer of Broken Walls,
Restorer of Streets with Dwellings.

¹³ "If you keep your feet from breaking the Sabbath
and from doing as you please on my holy day,
if you call the Sabbath a delight
and the Lord's holy day honorable,
and if you honor it by not going your own way
and not doing as you please or speaking idle words,
¹⁴ then you will find your joy in the Lord,
and I will cause you to ride in triumph on the heights of the land
and to feast on the inheritance of your father Jacob."
For the mouth of the Lord has spoken.

Fasting can be powerful, but God prefers a consistent daily walk of obedience. Specifically, God calls us to:

- Do away with the yoke of oppression.
- Stop the pointing finger and malicious talk.
- Get involved in helping the hungry and oppressed.
- Keep the Sabbath, delighting in it and honoring it by not going our own way.
- Be careful with our speech and not speak idle words.

Then God promises:

- That our light will rise in the darkness.
- That our night will become like noonday.

- To always guide us.
- To satisfy our needs in the desert.
- To strengthen us.
- To make us a well-watered garden; a spring whose waters never fail.
- To help us rebuild and restore what has been ruined.
- That we will find our joy in the Lord.
- To ride in triumph on the heights of the land.
- To feast on the inheritance of our forefathers.

Conclusion

This is not intended to be a comprehensive study on fasting or a practical how-to guide; there are excellent books and resources available online for that purpose. My hope is to introduce you to Jesus' teachings on fasting and encourage you to fast in a manner that pleases God. If fasting has not been a part of your spiritual life, pray about it, and be obedient to what God tells you to do. It can be a very rich experience!

11

Faith

Matthew 8, 9 & 14

Walking with Jesus is a walk of faith; Paul adds hope and love as the foundations of the Christian life. In a sense, they form a trinity; like the godhead, there is an intimate connection between the three.

Faith, Hope & Love

And now these three remain: faith, hope and love. But the greatest of these is love (1 Cor. 13:13).

Faith is confidence in (being sure of) what we hope for, the conviction of things not seen. AMP: *Faith is the assurance (the confirmation, the title deed) of the things [we] hope for* (Heb. 11:1). Both faith and hope involve intangibles: The things we hope for are in the future; faith involves what we don't see or cannot confirm with our senses—what God has said, the saving work of Christ, the fact that God exists. Our knowledge of God and his Word gives assurance that our hope is real. The two work hand in hand.

Our love for God and others is the tangible expression of what we believe and hope for. Our relationships are enriched and strengthened by our hope and faith: *Love always protects, always trusts, always hopes, always perseveres* (1 Cor. 13:7). Perseverance is an important part of all three.

But since we belong to the day, let us be sober, putting on faith and love as a breastplate, and the hope of salvation as a helmet (1 Thess. 5:8). The three form essential parts of our spiritual armor. Faith and love protect our hearts, while the hope of eternal salvation protects our thoughts. Without that helmet, faith and love can become selfish or misguided. Hope keeps our thoughts clear and focused on our salvation, guiding the rest of our lives.

We have heard of your faith in Christ Jesus and of the love you have for all God's people— the faith and love that spring from the hope stored up for you in heaven (Col. 1:4–5). Their faith and love are noteworthy—both flow out of the hope awakened by the gospel. Hope comes first; then faith appropriates these:

- The invisible reality of freedom from sin that we receive through Christ's sacrifice.
- A love relationship with God.
- Peace with others.
- Joy.

As a result, love for God and others flows from us.

A book could easily be written about faith, but it really isn't that complicated. These examples show the simplicity of walking with Christ in faith. You can do it!

A leper healed (Matthew 8)

[1] *When Jesus came down from the mountainside, large crowds followed him.* [2] *A man with leprosy came and knelt before him and said, "Lord, if you are willing, you can make me clean."*

³ Jesus reached out his hand and touched the man. "I am willing," he said. "Be clean!" Immediately he was cleansed of his leprosy.⁴ Then Jesus said to him, "See that you don't tell anyone. But go, show yourself to the priest and offer the gift Moses commanded, as a testimony to them."

This is child-like faith, which pleases God. It is a very simple faith, but with that mustard seed faith, the leper was healed. The man did not have to pray fervently or declare a healing. So how did he express his faith?

1.   He had heard about Jesus and sought him out. It did not matter what other people said or that he might be shunned for being unclean. Faith begins with a desire to be close to Jesus, in his presence. It is hard to have faith when you are preoccupied with worldly things or far from the Lord.

2.   He knelt before him, humbling himself and confessing his dependence on Jesus for something that to him was impossible. Worship strengthens faith and demonstrates submission to Jesus' lordship.

3.   He had simple faith that Jesus could heal him. He may have seen other miracles or heard Jesus teach, and was confident that healing was possible. It all depended on what Jesus wanted to do, not how much faith he had.

4.   He acknowledged Jesus' sovereignty and freedom to choose to heal or not. It is often taught that to pray "if it is your will" betrays a lack of faith, but Jesus honored that submission.

5.   He didn't always do this, but Jesus reached out and touched the man (exposing himself to possible contagion of leprosy), and the man was instantly healed.

The faith of the centurion

⁵ When Jesus had entered Capernaum, a centurion came to him, asking for help.

Once again, the first sign of faith is approaching Jesus and asking for his help. Prayer is a crucial part of the walk of faith.

⁶ "Lord," he said, "my servant lies at home paralyzed, suffering terribly."

No miracle was requested; he simply communicated the need, and, implicitly, his inability to do anything about it.

⁷ Jesus said to him, "I will come and heal him."

Jesus gave his word: in response to that faith, he would heal the servant. The man's simple faith touched him, and the centurion now has the Lord's promise.

⁸ The centurion replied, "Lord, I do not deserve to have you come under my roof. But just say the word, and my servant will be healed. ⁹ For I myself am a man under authority, with soldiers under me. I tell this one, 'Go,' and he goes; and that one, 'Come,' and he comes. I say to my servant, 'Do this,' and he does it."

This is faith: humility, believing Jesus' word, and understanding the nature of authority. The Roman Empire gave the centurion authority. By himself, he had no power to make his soldiers do anything, but they knew he had received authority from the emperor. They feared and respected that authority, and without argument or delay, did whatever was asked of them. They responded to their superior's words. The centurion knew that Jesus only had to say the word, and it would be done; he recognized the authority Jesus had received from his Father.

10 When Jesus heard this, he was amazed and said to those following him, "Truly I tell you, I have not found anyone in Israel with such great faith. 11 I say to you that many will come from the east and the west, and will take their places at the feast with Abraham, Isaac and Jacob in the kingdom of heaven. 12 But the subjects of the kingdom will be thrown outside, into the darkness, where there will be weeping and gnashing of teeth."

Jesus called that "great faith;" more faith than he had found in any Jew (this man was a Roman gentile). Jesus was amazed at his faith and was moved to respond to it. What would show you that someone has great faith? Here, it was the profound conviction that Jesus was under his Father's authority, having received it directly from God himself. The person who lacks that faith not only fails to receive miracles but will be cast into hell.

13 Then Jesus said to the centurion, "Go! Let it be done just as you believed it would." And his servant was healed at that moment.

What an interesting word! *"Let it be done just as you believed it would."* If you have faith for small things, you will receive small things. If you have mountain-moving faith, if you truly believe that Jesus, who created this world, has the power to move mountains, the mountain will move!

Fear quenches the disciples' faith

23 Then he got into the boat and his disciples followed him. 24 Suddenly a furious storm came up on the lake, so that the waves swept over the boat. But Jesus was sleeping. 25 The disciples went and woke him, saying, "Lord, save us! We're going to drown!"

Once again, the disciples went to Jesus; actually, they ran to him in a panic. They believed he could save them, and they asked for that, but they were also afraid. Fear is the opposite of faith. Fear paralyzes faith and robs us of it. These were Jesus' disciples; he expected more of them–more than he expected of a Roman centurion–which led to Jesus' rebuke:

²⁶ He replied, "You of little faith, why are you so afraid?"

If you have faith, there is no reason to be afraid. It is possible to have great faith or little faith. The disciples' fear betrayed their small faith. What part does fear play in your life? Does it betray your lack of faith? Or do you have a steady confidence that Jesus can manage all of the storms of life?

Then he got up and rebuked the winds and the waves, and it was completely calm.

Thank God, despite their little faith, Jesus still did a miracle; he was not about to let them die in that storm. Sometimes God does a miracle, not *because* of our *great* faith, but *despite* our *little* faith.

²⁷ The men were amazed and asked, "What kind of man is this? Even the winds and the waves obey him!"

Faith comes by hearing, and hearing by the word of God (Rom. 10:17). When we grow in our knowledge of Christ, our faith will grow as well. It is evident that they still lacked a clear concept of who Jesus was.

Touching the hem of his garment (Matthew 9)

¹⁸ While he was saying this, a synagogue leader came and knelt before him and said, "My daughter has just died. But come and put your hand on her, and she will live."

Here it is again! The man sought Jesus out, came to him, knelt, shared his need, made his request, and expressed his faith that Jesus could heal his daughter. He lacked the leper's humility to say "if you want to," or the humility of the centurion who felt he was unworthy to have Jesus enter his house. This was a synagogue leader who was bold enough to almost command Jesus what to do: "Come and put your hand on her!" His faith was impressive. The girl was dead, but he believed Jesus could resurrect her. There are various ways to come to Jesus, and he honored each of these requests.

¹⁹ Jesus got up and went with him, and so did his disciples.

Jesus was in the middle of a teaching, but without saying a word, he immediately got up and went with the man. On the way, we have another expression of faith:

²⁰ Just then a woman who had been subject to bleeding for twelve years came up behind him and touched the edge of his cloak. ²¹ She said to herself, "If I only touch his cloak, I will be healed."

²² Jesus turned and saw her. "Take heart, daughter," he said, "your faith has healed you." And the woman was healed at that moment.

Once again, the person approached Jesus, but she was so ashamed of her uncleanness that she could not work up the courage to ask him for anything. Her only expression of faith was the certainty that touching the edge of his cloak would be enough to heal her. And that was enough faith; Jesus clearly says: *"Your faith has healed you."*

The dead girl's father was probably anxious about this delay, but they finally got to his house:

²³ When Jesus entered the synagogue leader's house and saw the noisy crowd and people playing pipes, ²⁴ he said, "Go away. The girl is not dead but asleep." But they laughed at him. ²⁵ After the crowd had been put outside, he went in and took the girl by the hand, and she got up. ²⁶ News of this spread through all that region.

We have seen two kinds of healings:

1. Twice, the person expressed faith for their own healing (the leper and the woman with bleeding, both were ritually unclean).

2. Twice, another person's faith resulted in the healing (this girl and the centurion's servant).

In this case, nothing more is said about the father's faith. Once Jesus decided to go with him, it was already accomplished. The mocking of the crowd did not affect the healing (or, actually, the resurrection). Jesus just took the girl's hand, and she got up.

Two blind men healed

As we walk with Jesus through these chapters of Matthew, there is a continual procession of needs and requests, and demonstrations of simple faith:

²⁷ As Jesus went on from there, two blind men followed him, calling out, "Have mercy on us, Son of David!"

This time, two blind men followed Jesus, calling out to him. They were not asking for healing, but rather for mercy or compassion.

²⁸ When he had gone indoors, the blind men came to him, and he asked them, "Do you believe that I am able to do this?"

"Yes, Lord," they replied.

Although there was no initial response, they persisted in following Jesus, even into the house, where they approached him. Jesus wanted to clarify what they are looking for: "What do you mean when you ask me for mercy? Why are you following me?" They needed to be more specific in their request if they wanted healing. Now they clearly stated that they believed Jesus could heal them.

²⁹ *Then he touched their eyes and said, "According to your faith let it be done to you."*

That simple confession was enough to move Jesus. They received *according to their faith*. If you have faith for something small, that is what you will receive. If it is mountain-moving faith, the mountains will move.

³⁰ *And their sight was restored. Jesus warned them sternly, "See that no one knows about this."* ³¹ *But they went out and spread the news about him all over that region.*

³² *While they were going out, a man who was demon-possessed and could not talk was brought to Jesus.* ³³ *And when the demon was driven out, the man who had been mute spoke. The crowd was amazed and said, "Nothing like this has ever been seen in Israel."*

In this case, the poor man could not even talk! He couldn't ask for anything! He may have been so bound up by the demon that he did not even have faith, but his companions did. Here again, they came to Jesus. There is no mention of them asking for anything; with that simple faith of bringing the man to Jesus, the Lord did the miracle.

Jesus can multiply the little you have (Matthew 14)

¹³ *When Jesus heard [about John the Baptist's beheading], he withdrew by boat privately to a solitary place.*

Jesus was in mourning and wanted to be alone, but:

Hearing of this, the crowds followed him on foot from the towns.
¹⁴ When Jesus landed and saw a large crowd, he had compassion
on them and healed their sick.

Once again, the people demonstrated their faith by seeking Jesus out. That faith touched his heart, and he healed the sick. But now there is a problem:

¹⁵ As evening approached, the disciples came to him and said,
"This is a remote place, and it's already getting late. Send the
crowds away, so they can go to the villages and buy themselves
some food."

¹⁶ Jesus replied, "They do not need to go away. You give them
something to eat."

¹⁷ "We have here only five loaves of bread and two fish," they
answered.

¹⁸ "Bring them here to me," he said.

The disciples could not see the opportunity to exercise their faith and supply the need. For them, the best option was to send the people away. They passed the responsibility onto the crowd ("They came out here without thinking about food? Let them go and find what they can! It's not our problem!"). But Jesus said they don't have to go away. People who are just beginning to walk with Christ should not be burdened with something that we, with a more mature faith, can handle. The crowd had faith for healing, but there was no evidence of faith for this kind of miracle.

This was a test of the disciples' faith. Jesus believed that with the faith they had, it would be possible to feed this multitude, but they lacked the eyes of faith to believe for a miracle and multiply the little they had. Are you facing something that seems impossible? Could it be a test of your faith?

The willingness to give Jesus what they had allowed him to do the miracle. Do you have something that Jesus needs? Could he be saying: "Bring it here to me?"

[19] And he directed the people to sit down on the grass. Taking the five loaves and the two fish and looking up to heaven, he gave thanks and broke the loaves. Then he gave them to the disciples, and the disciples gave them to the people. [20] They all ate and were satisfied, and the disciples picked up twelve basketfuls of broken pieces that were left over. [21] The number of those who ate was about five thousand men, besides women and children.

How did Jesus do the miracle? There is no logical explanation, but we can follow the steps:

- He directed the people to sit down. He prepared the setting and organized the people.

- He took what he had and looked to heaven with faith and expectancy.

- He blessed and gave thanks for what he had.

- He gave the bread and fish to the disciples, and they passed them out. Imagine how their faith grew when they saw that bread and fish feed thousands!

When Jesus performs a miracle, he wants us to be satisfied and left with an abundance. We do not see many miracles of this nature today, but do you have faith that Jesus could do it again?

An opportunity and a test for Peter

22 Immediately Jesus made the disciples get into the boat and go on ahead of him to the other side, while he dismissed the crowd.

We already saw one test with the feeding of the multitude. Maybe the disciples felt they could relax now, but Jesus had another test of their faith, and another opportunity to grow in it. He sent them off alone in the boat while he dismissed the crowd.

You may be just coming out of a great test of your faith and want to rest for a while. However, it may be that Jesus has another test for you, based on the growth you have just experienced. Is something happening in your life that makes you feel like Jesus has abandoned you? Can you see a purpose Jesus might have in this test?

23 After he had dismissed them, he went up on a mountainside by himself to pray. Later that night, he was there alone, 24 and the boat was already a considerable distance from land, buffeted by the waves because the wind was against it.

Where was Jesus? Praying! All night! When Jesus is not in the boat with you, you may be buffeted by all kinds of things!

25 Shortly before dawn Jesus went out to them, walking on the lake.

Jesus left them on that lake, fighting with the wind and the waves all night long!

26 When the disciples saw him walking on the lake, they were terrified. "It's a ghost," they said, and cried out in fear.

27 But Jesus immediately said to them: "Take courage! It is I. Don't be afraid."

It's normal to be afraid in a test, but you don't have to be afraid of Jesus! He doesn't want to scare you! If you are in a storm right now, Jesus is with you, and his word is: *"Take courage! It is I. Don't be afraid."*

[28] *"Lord, if it's you," Peter replied, "tell me to come to you on the water."*

[29] *"Come," he said.*

Then Peter got down out of the boat, walked on the water and came toward Jesus.

Without considering everything involved, there was one thing in Peter's heart: he wanted to be with Jesus. He believes that if Christ could walk on water, he could too. However, only if it is truly Jesus; the faith must be in something solid, like Christ. And we have to wait for Jesus' word before we get out of the boat. When he gets that word, Peter gets out of the boat and walks.

[30] *But when he saw the wind, he was afraid and, beginning to sink, cried out, "Lord, save me!"*

[31] *Immediately Jesus reached out his hand and caught him. "You of little faith," he said, "why did you doubt?"*

In our experience today, it seems that Peter had great faith to get out of the boat and walk on water, especially given the wind and waves. However, Jesus rebuked him for his doubts and little faith. Jesus was saying that no matter how impossible something might look, how strong the wind might be, if we believe, nothing is difficult or impossible. Fear, doubts, and focusing on the circumstances steal those blessings. Jesus did not rebuke him for being presumptuous—he encouraged him and supported him in this step of faith. And he did not let him sink; he rescued him.

³² And when they climbed into the boat, the wind died down. ³³ Then those who were in the boat worshiped him, saying, "Truly you are the Son of God."

Are you getting beaten up by the winds and waves? Jesus wants to calm the storm and get into your boat. He really is the Son of God and is worthy of all your worship!

³⁴ When they had crossed over, they landed at Gennesaret. ³⁵ And when the men of that place recognized Jesus, they sent word to all the surrounding country. People brought all their sick to him ³⁶ and begged him to let the sick just touch the edge of his cloak, and all who touched it were healed.

This chapter of Matthew's Gospel (and this chapter on faith) ends with even more expressions of faith. The people recognized Jesus and knew that he had been sent by God with divine power. The word spread, inviting the people to have faith to come and receive, and in faith they brought *all* their sick. People came to Jesus with their needs. They asked for his touch, for his miracle. They made their request, their prayer, and reached out to touch him. Like the woman, they had faith that just touching the hem of his garment would bring healing. And *everyone* with the faith to touch him was healed.

That's it, that simple. There really is nothing complicated about faith. You have read the Bible. You know who Jesus is, and you are growing in your knowledge of him. You have probably accepted him as your Lord and Savior. You may have told others about him. What need can you bring to Jesus right now? Is there someone you can bring to him? Have you told Jesus about your request or need? Do you have the faith to touch him? If so, Jesus says that the one who believes will receive, according to their faith. Believe in Jesus with the same faith we have seen over and over again in this chapter. And don't doubt, like Peter did, and be rebuked by Jesus for your little faith.

12

Putting Faith in Practice
John 4:43-54; 5:1-18

In the previous chapter we saw various people healed in response to their faith. If we are going to walk as Jesus walked, we need to exercise our faith to minister to others and encourage them to release God's power through their faith. Faith is not a vague concept; it is something we must put into practice.

Long-distance healing

⁴³ After the two days he left for Galilee. ⁴⁴ (Now Jesus himself had pointed out that a prophet has no honor in his own country.) ⁴⁵ When he arrived in Galilee, the Galileans welcomed him. They had seen all that he had done in Jerusalem at the Passover Festival, for they also had been there.

Jesus had spent two amazing days with the Samaritans. It all started with a God-directed conversation with a woman of ill repute who brought the whole village to hear him. They were so hungry for the Word that they begged him to stay longer. For the first time, people embraced Jesus for who he was: the Messiah *("we have heard for ourselves, and we know that this man really is the Savior of the world" Jn. 4:42).* Unfortunately, that was not the case back home. Sure, the Galileans welcomed him, not as their savior, but because of the miracles he had performed, which many had witnessed during Passover in Jerusalem. There is no mention of miracles done in Samaria, nor were any requested.

Jesus pointed out something that many of us have experienced: a prophet is not honored in his own country (Mk. 6:4 adds: *among his relatives and in his own home*). They know you and your family. They went to school with you and work with you. It is much harder to gain their respect and honor. Thank God if your own people welcome you, but if not, don't let it bother you. Jesus wasn't either.

Honor

Baker's Evangelical Dictionary of Biblical Theology states:

"To honor someone is to give weight or to grant a person a position of respect and even authority in one's life. A person grants honor most frequently on the basis of position, status, or wealth, but it can and should also be granted on the basis of character. Honor is an internal attitude of respect, courtesy, and reverence, it should be accompanied by appropriate attention or even obedience."

God places a high value on honor:

- We are commanded to honor our parents if we want a good, long life.

- Jesus quotes Isaiah: *"'These people honor me with their lips, but their hearts are far from me. They worship me in vain; their teachings are merely human rules'"* (Matt. 15:8–9). The Galileans may have honored Jesus with their lips, but he knew that their hearts were far from him. It is possible to give the appearance of honoring God (or another person), but if it is not from the heart, it is in vain.

- Jesus said: *"My Father will honor the one who serves me (John 12:26)."* What a privilege to be honored by God! If you are serving Jesus, you can expect that honor.

Are you honoring God? His servants? Your parents? If you are truly honoring the Lord, you will be blessed, and the Father will honor you. Are you receiving the honor you deserve?

A request from a royal official

46 Once more he visited Cana in Galilee, where he had turned the water into wine. And there was a certain royal official whose son lay sick at Capernaum. 47 When this man heard that Jesus had arrived in Galilee from Judea, he went to him and begged him to come and heal his son, who was close to death.

Jesus went straight to a town where he should be well received— by now, everyone knew about the wine at the wedding feast. They were like family, but they couldn't see beyond the wine. If he were hoping for a rest after the long walk from Samaria, he would be disappointed. The good news is that a prominent official, a member of the king's court, had heard about Jesus. What a contrast from the despised Samaritans! But Jesus was no politician and was in no rush to gain the support of this influential man. Furthermore, it was about an eighteen-mile (30 km) walk from Cana to Capernaum, after having just walked from Samaria.

48 "Unless you people see signs and wonders," Jesus told him, "you will never believe."

Jesus is compassionate, loving, and always ready to help us, right? Sure! But Jesus also had boundaries, and here, when he heard that this poor boy was about to die, he seemed cold-hearted. Why?

Jesus had just come from Samaria—a place supposedly closed to the truth, where he was received gladly and never was asked for a special sign. Jesus was tired of people who always wanted something from him, but were uninterested in getting to know him or listening to his word. This poor man and his sick son bore the brunt of his frustration.

Do you think Jesus is frustrated today with so many people clamoring for a miracle or blessing? Could he long to be truly honored, from the heart, by people who just want to be with him, without asking for some sign or wonder? Do you need signs and wonders, emotional worship services, or some special spiritual experience to keep your faith going? Or can you simply believe in him for who he is?

Jesus gives the word

⁴⁹ The royal official said, "Sir, come down before my child dies." ⁵⁰ "Go," Jesus replied, "your son will live."

Sometimes an unanswered prayer can be a test. How persistent will this man be? God honors our perseverance in prayer. It could be a life-or-death situation for a child or a friend. Are you willing to devote the time and energy necessary to persuade Jesus to act?

After traveling from Judea to Galilee, Jesus didn't feel like walking 18 more miles, and he didn't need to! Jesus does not have to be physically present, or pray, or touch the sick person. With a word, it was done! That was a whole lot easier! Do you believe Jesus can do the same for family members in other cities or countries? Or someone in prison?

However, as is almost always the case, there is a condition: the father must go. That's it. It doesn't take much faith, just obedience. Fortunately, *the man took Jesus at his word and departed.*

If the father didn't believe Jesus and didn't go, it is very possible the boy would have died. To stay and keep begging Jesus to go with him, or to get angry about his refusal to go, would be doubting Jesus' word—and he might lose his son. We need to trust what Jesus said in the Bible, as well as what he says today. Do you take Jesus at his word? Is there some simple word you need to obey? Jesus can move mountains right now, in the Spirit. It doesn't matter how hard or how far it might be.

The first healing

⁵¹ While he was still on the way, his servants met him with the news that his boy was living.

What was that father thinking on the way home? Was he praising the Lord? Fighting doubt? Hurrying as fast as he could? We don't know, but he had good news waiting for him: His boy was alive!

Are you waiting for some good news? That your son got saved? Your mother got healed? Could it be that the next phone call or Email could be that good news? What is your request to the Lord? How is your faith?

⁵² When he inquired as to the time when his son got better, they said to him, "Yesterday, at one in the afternoon, the fever left him." ⁵³ Then the father realized that this was the exact time at which Jesus had said to him, "Your son will live." So he and his whole household believed.

Of course, when God does such an amazing miracle, the whole family believes! And that is what God wants! Why wouldn't he want to glorify himself?

⁵⁴ This was the second sign Jesus performed after coming from Judea to Galilee.

It sounds like this was his second sign after returning from Judea on this trip, but it probably refers to the second sign John records, with Cana being the first.

Bethesda

⁵:¹Some time later, Jesus went up to Jerusalem for one of the Jewish festivals.

How much later we do not know, but Jesus is on the road again. This time it doesn't say he had to go through Samaria; he probably took the usual road on the east side of the Jordan.

² Now there is in Jerusalem near the Sheep Gate a pool, which in Aramaic is called Bethesda and which is surrounded by five covered colonnades. ³ Here a great number of disabled people used to lie—the blind, the lame, the paralyzed—and they waited for the moving of the waters.

When you visit a great city, where do you go first? The tourist places? Museums? Good restaurants? A well-known church?

Jesus went to Bethesda. There is a beautiful fountain in New York's Central Park called Bethesda, adorned with angels. At first, this colonnaded pool also sounds pretty, but the angel was the only nice thing about it. The air was full of groaning and crying, and the stench of excrement, urine, and the ulcers of the sick people. You could barely see the putrid water through the multitude of every kind of disabled person.

Jesus went straight to Bethesda because he loves to heal and minister to desperate people forgotten by the world. Where is Bethesda in your city? A hospital? A park? Some shelter?

⁴ From time to time an angel of the Lord would come down and stir up the waters. The first one into the pool after each such disturbance would be cured of whatever disease they had.

Many manuscripts do not even include this verse, which may have been added to explain why people waited for the waters to move. We do not know precisely what happened there, but the angel likely did not appear physically. The Bible neither affirms nor condemns the legend. There are countless stories of healings at special places, with holy water, or on some pilgrimage. It is possible that people with genuine faith may get healed, regardless of whether the water is actually blessed or not. It may have just been a superstition, but it was the only hope for these people. There was a problem for many of them, though: if you were paralyzed, there was no way to get to the water fast enough. If you were blind, how would you know where to go?

⁵ One who was there had been an invalid for thirty-eight years.

Thirty-eight years is a long time; this man may have been among the oldest at Bethesda. How long have you been battling some problem in your life?

Do you want to get well?

⁶ When Jesus saw him lying there and learned that he had been in this condition for a long time, he asked him, "Do you want to get well?"

Bethesda was crowded with invalids that day, but Jesus saw only this man. He didn't always heal everyone. If we have a healing service, it may be that he chooses just one person to heal.

Possibly it was by divine revelation; somehow Jesus learned how long this man had been ill and asked what seems like an obvious question: "Do you want to get well?" Isn't that why he is there? Who doesn't want to get well? But Jesus knows that some people become accustomed to being sick and resist seeking the help they need to find wholeness. Some have simply lost all hope of a better life. It can happen in a marriage, with some sin, or in your economic situation. It feels like nobody sees you, and God does not realize how much you are suffering. You don't have the faith to believe for a miracle, or maybe you have your hopes fixed on something as nebulous as the moving of the water, something that has not worked for thirty-eight years. This may be your day for a miracle.

What is your excuse?

[7] "Sir," the invalid replied, "I have no one to help me into the pool when the water is stirred. While I am trying to get in, someone else goes down ahead of me."

Somebody gets there before me. Someone else always gets the prophecy. The evangelist always prays for another person. Someone is always ahead of me.

Excuses can blind us to new possibilities and trap us with logic. This man does not know how to respond to Jesus' question. He can only see one alternative, and all the reasons why that would be impossible.

What is your excuse? What is your circumstance that makes it seem impossible to receive a miracle?

[8] Then Jesus said to him, "Get up! Pick up your mat and walk."

Jesus paid no attention to his excuses, and thankfully did not deny him a miracle because of his lack of faith. This man had no idea who Jesus was and appeared to lack any faith; apparently, faith is not a prerequisite to receiving a miracle. This was Jesus' sovereign choice, but there are three things the man had to do to get his miracle:

- Get up
- Pick up his mat, the symbol of his shame and pain
- Walk

For most people, that would be simple, but for thirty-eight years, this man has not been able to walk. Jesus does not pray for him. He does not touch him. The paralyzed man had to act in faith and do what he had been unable to do for thirty-eight years.

Sadly, many people are stuck at Bethesda, holding on to a vague hope, yet unable to move on with their lives. They may be there for years, paralyzed by fear and the past, bound by the enemy. Sometimes we need the faith to get up and get moving. Both these miracles involved movement. Are there times we do too much waiting, and just need to get up and get going?

The second healing

The first healing was long-distance, with a simple word from Jesus, followed by a father's obedience. This healing is a command given in faith and knowledge of God's sovereign will. Why is it so difficult for us to follow Jesus' model? Didn't he say we would do the works he did—and greater? Do we lack the faith? Why is it that we rarely give people these simple tests of obedience and faith? Why is it that we have to pray and declare and agonize for days to see a healing? Could it be that we are not in touch with the Spirit, not paying attention to what he is telling us to do? Or perhaps a lack of faith?

⁹ At once the man was cured; he picked up his mat and walked.

Out of that whole crowd, Jesus chose just one man to heal. He did not preach to them or give an invitation for healing, as we might expect to do. We have taught that Jesus wants to heal everyone, but apparently that is not always the case.

With that first step of faith ("Get up!"), the man was healed, and obeyed Jesus and walked. In an instant, his life was transformed. After being paralyzed for thirty-eight years, you would expect him to need some therapy and time to strengthen his legs, but when Jesus heals, it is a total healing. Do you know someone who needs a total transformation? Are you like this man, full of excuses and logic?

- "I've never seen that kind of healing."
- "That was Jesus; we can't expect the same thing."
- "A healing like this is very rare."
- "I don't want to give someone false hope or play with their feelings."

Both of these healings involved movement. Sometimes we simply need to leave behind the things of the past that have held us paralyzed and get out of bed, leave the house, turn off the internet, and walk with Jesus.

Can you heal on the Sabbath?

There was just one problem with what Jesus did: it was on the Sabbath.

The day on which this took place was a Sabbath, [10] *and so the Jewish leaders said to the man who had been healed, "It is the Sabbath; the law forbids you to carry your mat."*

Unfortunately, there are Christians like these leaders, always looking for something to criticize. Instead of rejoicing in the man's healing, they condemn him. It did not fit their religious framework, although carrying a mat was not forbidden in the law. Is that to say that the Sabbath was unimportant to Jesus? No way! He kept the Sabbath. But religion exists to bless us; we don't exist to serve a religion. Sometimes our religion can keep us from experiencing a miracle.

11 But he replied, "The man who made me well said to me, 'Pick up your mat and walk.' " 12 So they asked him, "Who is this fellow who told you to pick it up and walk?" 13 The man who was healed had no idea who it was, for Jesus had slipped away into the crowd that was there.

The person without faith will look for picky details, but this man does not even know who healed him!

14 Later Jesus found him at the temple and said to him, "See, you are well again. Stop sinning or something worse may happen to you."

He went straight to the temple to thank God! That is great, but Jesus' words sound harsh. He implies that it could have been sin that resulted in his sickness, but God had mercifully healed him. Now he needed to repent, or something worse could happen (which indeed occurs far too frequently). God heals, saves, and restores, but if the person does not repent, they end up worse than before. Like a person delivered from evil spirits, he must be filled with the Holy Spirit, or the demon could return with even worse demons.

God's word for you

I believe there are some important things God wants to speak to your life:

- Do you have an ill family member, perhaps in another place? Do you have faith that God can heal or touch their life?

- Is God calling you to take some step of faith?

- Is it time for you to get up and put aside resentment, anger, and excuses? Is it time to get moving in the power of God?

- Is there some sickness, sin, or habit that seems impossible for you to overcome? You may have been fighting it a long time. Have you been focused on the wrong thing, like the movement of the waters?

- Do you want to get well? Honestly, do you want to be saved, healed, and set free?

- Are you playing with God? Has God done miracles in your life, but you still have not repented? Don't delay, or something worse could happen to you or your family.

13

What is Hope?

The dictionary defines "hope" as: "to cherish a desire with anticipation; to want something to happen or be true; a feeling of expectation and desire for a particular thing to happen." We talk a lot about hope: "I hope it doesn't rain on the picnic," "I hope I get that raise." But those are just wishes over which we have no control; there is no certainty that things will go in our favor.

Biblical hope is very different:

- A trustful expectation, particularly with reference to the fulfillment of God's promises. Hope is the anticipation of a favorable outcome under God's guidance; the confidence that what God has done for us in the past guarantees our participation in what God will do in the future. (*Holman Bible Dictionary*)

- A strong, positive, and confident expectation of future reward.

Secular dictionaries consider these definitions "archaic," outdated, and no longer relevant to today's world. I believe that this hope is exactly what we need!

True Hope

The Christian's hope is *in* God, and comes *from* God: *Yes, my soul, find rest in God; my hope comes from him* (Ps. 62:5).

You don't have to work up hope. God *gives* you hope based on the good plans he has for your life: *For I know the plans I have for you," declares the LORD, "plans to prosper you and not to harm you, plans to give you hope and a future* (Jer. 29:11).

Our hope is based on what the Bible says:

- *May those who fear you rejoice when they see me, for I have put my hope in your word* (Ps. 119:74).

- *For everything that was written in the past was written to teach us, so that through the endurance taught in the Scriptures and the encouragement they provide, we might have hope* (Rom. 15:4). Others' past experiences and God's promises for the future provide the encouragement to endure and keep hope strong.

- Paul had hope in promises made to previous generations, specifically regarding the resurrection: *And now it is because of my hope in what God has promised our ancestors that I am on trial today* (Acts 26:6). Paul's hope was strong enough to enable him to endure countless beatings, imprisonment, and eventually, death.

The Bible promises that if you know God, your hope is not in vain: *Then you will know that I am the LORD; those who hope in me will not be disappointed* (Is. 49:23).

Against all hope, Abraham in hope believed and so became the father of many nations, just as it had been said to him, "So shall your offspring be." Without weakening in his faith, he faced the fact that his body was as good as dead—since he was about a hundred years old—and that Sarah's womb was also dead (Rom. 4:18–19). It was faith in God's promise and the thought of future generations that gave Abraham hope. That hope quickened his faith for God to do the impossible. All the evidence was stacked against hope, yet his faith was strong enough to overcome the facts and wait for the fulfillment of God's promise.

False Hope

Hope is not limited to Christians. As opposed to the certainty of our hope, based on our faith in God, the hope of the godless is very ethereal: *Such is the destiny of all who forget God; so perishes the hope of the godless* (Job 8:13).

As opposed to the joy awaiting those who hope in God, there is emptiness for the godless: *The prospect of the righteous is joy, but the hopes of the wicked come to nothing* (Prov . 10:28).

What a tragedy to place all your hope in something that cannot deliver on its promises.

- Many things look strong and promising: *A horse is a vain hope for deliverance; despite all its great strength it cannot save* (Ps. 33:17).

- Those who put their hope in the stock market or real estate may be sadly disappointed, yet many continue to put their hopes in money: *Command those who are rich in this present world not to be arrogant nor to put their hope in wealth, which is so uncertain, but to put their hope in God, who richly provides us with everything for our enjoyment* (1 Tim. 6:17). It is easier to hope in God if you have nothing else; when you have great wealth or other resources it is very tempting to place your hopes in them.

Spiritual leaders often promote false hope: *This is what the LORD Almighty says: "Do not listen to what the prophets are prophesying to you; they fill you with false hopes. They speak visions from their own minds, not from the mouth of the LORD* (Jer. 23:16).

Benefits of Hope

- Physical and emotional health; those who fail to see hope fulfilled may suffer physically and emotionally: *Hope deferred makes the heart sick, but a longing fulfilled is a tree of life* (Prov. 13:12).

- When hope is gone, we may feel as Israel did, dried up and cut off: *Then he said to me: "Son of man, these bones are the people of Israel. They say, 'Our bones are dried up and our hope is gone; we are cut off.'* (Ez. 37:11).

- Energy and strength: *Those who hope in (or wait on) the Lord will renew their strength. They will soar on wings like eagles; they will run and not grow weary, they will walk and not be faint* (Is. 40:31).

- Boldness: *And if what was transitory came with glory, how much greater is the glory of that which lasts! Therefore, since we have such a hope, we are very bold* (2 Cor. 3:11-12).

- Motivation to serve God: *That is why we labor and strive, because we have put our hope in the living God, who is the Savior of all people, and especially of those who believe* (1 Tim. 4:10).

- Encouragement: *God did this so that, by two unchangeable things in which it is impossible for God to lie, we who have fled to take hold of the hope set before us may be greatly encouraged* (Heb. 6:18).

- Stability: *We have this hope as an anchor for the soul, firm and secure* (Heb. 6:19).

- Endurance: *We remember before our God and Father your work produced by faith, your labor prompted by love, and your endurance inspired by hope in our Lord Jesus Christ* (1 Thess. 1:3).

- Cleansing: *Dear friends, now we are children of God, and what we will be has not yet been made known. But we know that when Christ appears, we shall be like him, for we shall see him as he is. All who have this hope in him purify themselves, just as he is pure* (1 Jn. 3:2–3).

What We Hope For

Christ's return: *While we wait for the blessed hope—the appearing of the glory of our great God and Savior, Jesus Christ* (Tit. 2:13). By its very nature, hope always involves waiting.

Eternal life: *So that, having been justified by his grace, we might become heirs having the hope of eternal life* (Tit. 3:7). Hope is a natural result of a saving relationship with Jesus Christ; experiencing God's grace in justification (being declared not guilty) forms the foundation for being children and heirs of God. That, in turn, gives us a firm hope in eternal life.

Grace: *Therefore, with minds that are alert and fully sober, set your hope on the grace to be brought to you when Jesus Christ is revealed at his coming* (1 Pet. 1:13). When Jesus returns, we will be beneficiaries of the fullness of God's unmerited favor.

Note that none of these are experienced in this life.

The Holy Spirit and Hope

When you are full of the Spirit and his power, you should overflow with hope. The foundation is faith, a faith which releases the God of hope to fill you with his joy and peace: *May the God of hope fill you with all joy and peace as you trust in him, so that you may overflow with hope by the power of the Holy Spirit* (Rom. 15:13).

Through the Spirit we eagerly await by faith the righteousness for which we hope (Gal. 5:5). Another focus of hope is righteousness. Again, waiting is involved, as is faith. But the Spirit gives you the grace and strength to wait and endure. There is a sense of excitement and anticipation, much like a child waiting for Christmas, as you *eagerly* await.

On our own, we cannot understand hope. It is revealed to us as the Spirit enlightens the eyes of our hearts: *I pray that the eyes of your heart may be enlightened in order that you may know the hope to which he has called you* (Eph. 1:18). *Not only so, but we ourselves, who have the firstfruits of the Spirit, groan inwardly as we wait eagerly for our adoption to sonship, the redemption of our bodies. For in this hope we were saved. But hope that is seen is no hope at all. Who hopes for what they already have? But if we hope for what we do not yet have, we wait for it patiently* (Rom. 8:23–25). Here again, as in Galatians, hope enables you to *eagerly* wait for what God has promised. Your salvation benefits you now, but as Paul says in 1 Corinthians 15, if you only had hope for this life, you would be most pitied of all men. The focus of your salvation is the hope of the amazing future God has prepared for you:

- The redemption of your body, glorified and free from all pain and sickness.
- Your adoption as sons and daughters, with all the privileges inherent as God's heirs.

The Holy Spirit is the deposit, guaranteeing and giving you a taste of future blessings. Sometimes it is hard to wait, and you groan, but if you have a strong and steady hope, you patiently and eagerly wait. Once you receive what you have hoped for, hope is no longer necessary. Hope always involves something you don't yet have.

Final Thoughts

Always be prepared to give an answer to everyone who asks you to give the reason for the hope that you have (1 Peter 3:15). To give the reason, we have to understand what that hope is. Do these Scriptures make it clearer to you? Can you explain the reason for your hope?

Nowhere in Scripture do we see hope referring to good things in this life, such as having hope that marital problems will be resolved. That hope is important, but Scriptural hope is focused on life after death. That hope can strengthen our faith in God's promises for our lives now. But, as opposed to the absolute certainty of the things God has promised us in the future, we have no guarantees in this life for healing of sickness, restored marriages, or children coming back to the Lord. It is our hope that gives us the grace to persevere in the midst of disappointment.

What have you learned here about hope? Have you been misled by false hope? How much do you think about the blessed hope of Christ's return and your life after death? Are you experiencing any of the benefits associated with that hope? Are you suffering because you have lost hope? How is your patience? Endurance? How would you say you are doing with faith, hope, and love?

I pray that the Holy Spirit will flood you with hope as you experience the peace and joy of the Lord and the sure confidence of what God has prepared for you.

14

There is Always Hope; it is Never too Late for Jesus

John 11

In this well-known story, we see a clear connection between faith and hope. It was a struggle for Martha and Mary to hold on to hope when everything seemed to say it was too late. Even when it seems that all hope is gone, Jesus wants to keep your faith and hope alive. As we saw in the chapters on faith, there was something simple they had to do to receive their miracle.

Where is your pain?

¹Now a man named Lazarus was sick. He was from Bethany, the village of Mary and her sister Martha.

Since we live in a fallen world under the influence of the evil one, life is full of sickness, suffering, and tragedy. Where is the pain in your life right now? Are you suffering? You could be in excellent health, but suffering from a broken heart, which is more painful than the worst headache. You are not alone. Problems are part of life. In this case, Lazarus was sick. When someone is ill, the whole family is affected, and Lazarus' sisters were also suffering.

This is the first mention of Lazarus in the Bible. He may have heard about Jesus from his sisters, but he had never met him.

Sometimes we have to hit bottom to finally call on Jesus. Do you know a Lazarus? Maybe in your own family? Or someone who needs Jesus?

² (This Mary, whose brother Lazarus now lay sick, was the same one who poured perfume on the Lord and wiped his feet with her hair.)

The only other reference to Mary and Martha is in Luke 10:38–42:

As Jesus and his disciples were on their way, he came to a village where a woman named Martha opened her home to him. She had a sister called Mary, who sat at the Lord's feet listening to what he said. But Martha was distracted by all the preparations that had to be made. She came to him and asked, "Lord, don't you care that my sister has left me to do the work by myself? Tell her to help me!"

"Martha, Martha," the Lord answered, "you are worried and upset about many things, but few things are needed—or indeed only one. Mary has chosen what is better, and it will not be taken away from her."

It was Martha who opened her home to Jesus and was busy preparing everything for him, but it was Mary who was remembered by John and mentioned as Lazarus' sister. Why? Because she sat at his feet and listened to him. Jesus said that is all that's needed. It is the better choice.

Have you made that choice? Are you a Martha, or a Mary?

- Do you get bothered by others who don't do enough to "serve" Jesus? Are you distracted?

- Do you really love Jesus?

- Are you worried and upset about many things, which rob you of your intimacy with Jesus? Do you feel overwhelmed by all the details?

- Have you chosen something that will be taken away from you?

After the miracle in this chapter, Mary anointed Jesus with perfume and dried his feet with her hair (Jn. 12:1–8). Are you more like Judas, who could only think about what a waste it was? Or are you able to express an exuberant love for Jesus?

Perhaps you have settled for something that doesn't truly satisfy. It is good to be busy in church, but it may be time to choose what is better. Sit at Jesus' feet. Listen to him. Pour out your love and gratitude to him in tearful worship.

Send Jesus a message (a prayer) to tell him about your need

Have you told Jesus where you are hurting? Have you given him your burdens? This was Mary and Martha's message:

³ So the sisters sent word to Jesus, "Lord, the one you love is sick."

They don't "declare" anything. They don't even ask for a miracle. They trust that Jesus will know what to do. They just want to let him know what is happening. Is there something you need to give to him, trusting that he will know what to do? He loves you, too. Are you aware of that love?

⁴ When he heard this, Jesus said, "This sickness will not end in death. No, it is for God's glory so that God's Son may be glorified through it."

God is in control! Could it be that Jesus wants to glorify himself in whatever problem you are facing? Do you have the faith to believe that Jesus knows the purpose of your trials? Are you willing to suffer so Jesus can glorify himself in your life?

Some sicknesses will end in death. If Jesus does not come first, someday you will die. If God has determined that a sickness will end in your death, you can declare healing and fervently pray all day, but most likely, you will still die.

⁵ Now Jesus loved Martha and her sister and Lazarus. ⁶ So when he heard that Lazarus was sick, he stayed where he was two more days.

That seems contradictory: Jesus loved them, but he didn't rush to comfort them and heal Lazarus. He could have saved them a lot of agony, to say nothing of Lazarus not having to die, but raising a dead man brings God far more glory than healing a common illness.

Does it seem like Jesus did not get your message or understand how urgent it is? Back then, there was no phone or internet. The sisters had no way of knowing if Jesus got their message or not. In faith, each day they wait for Jesus to come. But he doesn't show up.

Jesus leaves for Lazarus' house

⁷ Then he said to his disciples, "Let us go back to Judea."

⁸ "But Rabbi," they said, "a short while ago the Jews there tried to stone you, and yet you are going back?"

⁹ Jesus answered, "Are there not twelve hours of daylight? Anyone who walks in the daytime will not stumble, for they see by this world's light. [10] *It is when a person walks at night that they stumble, for they have no light."*

Is your life ruled by circumstances? By the fears, warnings, and threats of other people? Are you walking in the daylight, with nothing to hide? Do you rely on the inner light God has given you? God has given us the sun and a brain to help us walk during the day. At night, if you don't have the Holy Spirit and the light of his Word, you will stumble. If you are walking through the valley of the shadow of death, do you have that inner light to guide you?

[11] *After he had said this, he went on to tell them, "Our friend Lazarus has fallen asleep; but I am going there to wake him up."*

[12] *His disciples replied, "Lord, if he sleeps, he will get better."* [13] *Jesus had been speaking of his death, but his disciples thought he meant natural sleep.*

[14] *So then he told them plainly, "Lazarus is dead,* [15] *and for your sake I am glad I was not there, so that you may believe. But let us go to him."*

[16] *Then Thomas (also known as Didymus) said to the rest of the disciples, "Let us also go, that we may die with him."*

This was also going to be a great lesson for the disciples. We tend to only think about ourselves. Can you see beyond yourself? Or are you like Thomas? Unable to see the possibilities, and trapped in unbelief?

Jesus said he was glad that he was not there to heal Lazarus, so that the disciples might believe. Could it be that Jesus has allowed the darkness in your life right now so that your faith might grow?

Does it seem like Jesus has shown up too late to help you?

¹⁷ On his arrival, Jesus found that Lazarus had already been in the tomb for four days. ¹⁸ Now Bethany was less than two miles from Jerusalem,¹⁹ and many Jews had come to Martha and Mary to comfort them in the loss of their brother.

Yes, Jesus arrived very late, but at least he had a big audience!

²⁰ When Martha heard that Jesus was coming, she went out to meet him, but Mary stayed at home.

²¹ "Lord," Martha said to Jesus, "if you had been here, my brother would not have died. ²² But I know that even now God will give you whatever you ask."

Mary was disappointed with Jesus, maybe even angry. She stayed home. Martha was less motivated by feelings, and felt obligated to do the right thing. She went out to meet Jesus. She did have faith; she believed Jesus could have healed her brother. She knew that the Father would give Jesus whatever he asked for, but that faith did not mean she would go to the tomb and declare a resurrection. She left the situation in Jesus' hands, even though she could not understand why Jesus did not come earlier. As we will see in verse 24, she did not expect a resurrection. Is there something in your life right now that you cannot understand? Why hasn't Jesus done more?

²³ Jesus said to her, "Your brother will rise again."

²⁴ Martha answered, "I know he will rise again in the resurrection at the last day."

[25] Jesus said to her, "I am the resurrection and the life. The one who believes in me will live, even though they die; [26] and whoever lives by believing in me will never die. Do you believe this?"

[27] "Yes, Lord," she replied, "I believe that you are the Messiah, the Son of God, who is to come into the world."

Like many of us, Martha had faith—but limited faith. She believed in life after death, that Jesus was the Messiah, and that he was God. However, her faith did not touch her current situation or her grief. She had a faith that is "out there," that was difficult to apply to her daily life. And that is true for many of us. We may have faith for others and faith for the future, but little faith for ourselves and our current problems. The good news is that our lack of faith doesn't limit Jesus. It is not about you, but about him: his love, mercy, and power.

Do you have dreams that have died? A ministry that has died? A dead marriage? Jesus is the resurrection and the life! He can bring new life to whatever has died!

Jesus calls you

[28] After she had said this, she went back and called her sister Mary aside. "The Teacher is here," she said, "and is asking for you." [29] When Mary heard this, she got up quickly and went to him. [30] Now Jesus had not yet entered the village, but was still at the place where Martha had met him. [31] When the Jews who had been with Mary in the house, comforting her, noticed how quickly she got up and went out, they followed her, supposing she was going to the tomb to mourn there.

[32] When Mary reached the place where Jesus was and saw him, she fell at his feet and said, "Lord, if you had been here, my brother would not have died."

33 When Jesus saw her weeping, and the Jews who had come along with her also weeping, he was deeply moved in spirit and troubled. 34 "Where have you laid him?" he asked.

"Come and see, Lord," they replied.

It doesn't say that Martha fell at Jesus' feet, but Mary did. She said the very same thing her sister said: "if you had been here."

- "If only you had come when I called, and healed my brother, everything would be fine!"
- "If you had changed my wife's heart, she would not be with that other man."
- "If you had healed my mother, she would still be alive."

Is there an "if only" you have for Jesus?

It may hurt so much that you don't want to go to church or see Jesus. You stay at home. But Jesus loves you and is calling you. Interestingly, Jesus didn't say anything to Mary. He loved her, and it hurt him to see her cry. Jesus is deeply moved by your anguish as well.

35 Jesus wept.

What have you buried? What is painful for you? Can you believe that Jesus cries with you? Take a moment, let the tears come, and draw close to Jesus to see his tears.

36 Then the Jews said, "See how he loved him!"

37 But some of them said, "Could not he who opened the eyes of the blind man have kept this man from dying?"

What kind of person are you? Do you see God's love in sending Jesus to earth to give us a new life? Are you amazed at his salvation? Or does it bother you that God does not do more to end the suffering in this world? Are there things you just do not understand about life or about God? What doesn't make sense to you?

Is there a stone you need to remove?

38 Jesus, once more deeply moved, came to the tomb. It was a cave with a stone laid across the entrance. 39 "Take away the stone," he said.

"But, Lord," said Martha, the sister of the dead man, "by this time there is a bad odor, for he has been there four days."

Jesus wanted to do a miracle. He did not need great proclamations of faith. He did not expect them to declare a resurrection. However, there was something they needed to do: take away the stone. It was not that hard. It did not require great faith, but at that moment, it was the last thing these sisters wanted to do. It was like opening an old wound, going back to see something that you buried and want to forget about.

Is there a stone you have to remove? Something that stinks? Something you know God wants you to do that just doesn't make any sense to you?

Do you want to see the glory of God?

40 Then Jesus said, "Did I not tell you that if you believe, you will see the glory of God?"

Jesus was not impressed with their excuse. He didn't deny that the smell would be bad, or that it would be hard for Mary and Martha. But faith, evidenced by their obedience, was necessary to see God's glory.

41 So they took away the stone. Then Jesus looked up and said, "Father, I thank you that you have heard me. 42 I knew that you always hear me, but I said this for the benefit of the people standing here, that they may believe that you sent me."

⁴³ When he had said this, Jesus called in a loud voice, "Lazarus, come out!"

The Father always hears your High Priest, interceding for you at his right hand.

⁴⁴ The dead man came out, his hands and feet wrapped with strips of linen, and a cloth around his face.

Jesus said to them, "Take off the grave clothes and let him go."

Sometimes Jesus does a miracle, but we leave the person bound up. We don't want to let him go. Are there some grave clothes you need to take off? Somebody you need to set free? Something you need to let go? When a new believer is "resurrected" from spiritual death, he may still be bound up by things of his past. He needs brothers and sisters to help him take off those things that are binding him. Don't leave him wrapped up in his grave clothes!

Mary and Martha went through hell. They may have been angry with Jesus. They could not understand why he would not come to help someone he loved. But it is never too late for Jesus. He is the resurrection and the life! There is hope for you. You do not need great faith, just mustard seed faith. Jesus may be calling you right now. He is crying with you. He is asking you to remove a stone that is keeping him from performing a miracle or setting someone free. He wants to glorify himself and do far more than you would expect in your wildest dreams.

15

Love: The Most Important

It is impossible to walk like Jesus without love. Paul said it is more important than faith or hope, and the biblical support for that is overwhelming. Everyone wants to be loved, and most want to love somebody. But what is love? Much of what passes for love in movies and on TV is just emotion and lust. The apostle Paul wrote in the famous love chapter (1 Cor. 13:1–7 and 13):

If I speak in the tongues of men or of angels, but do not have love, I am only a resounding gong or a clanging cymbal. If I have the gift of prophecy and can fathom all mysteries and all knowledge, and if I have a faith that can move mountains, but do not have love, I am nothing. If I give all I possess to the poor and give over my body to hardship that I may boast, but do not have love, I gain nothing.

Love is patient, love is kind. It does not envy, it does not boast, it is not proud. It does not dishonor others, it is not self-seeking, it is not easily angered, it keeps no record of wrongs. Love does not delight in evil but rejoices with the truth. It always protects, always trusts, always hopes, always perseveres. And now these three remain: faith, hope and love. But the greatest of these is love.

Yes, the greatest is love. Jesus made an impressive statement about love when he responded to the question raised by a teacher of the law:

"Teacher, which is the greatest commandment in the Law?"

Jesus replied: "'Love the Lord your God with all your heart and with all your soul and with all your mind.' This is the first and greatest commandment. And the second is like it: 'Love your neighbor as yourself.' All the Law and the Prophets hang on these two commandments" (Matt. 22:36–40).

If we are going to walk like Jesus walked, we have to love like Jesus loved. Love must be the distinguishing characteristic of our lives. The sinner does not love naturally; he only thinks about what is important to him, because by nature we are self-centered. We start to truly love only after experiencing God's great love:

And so we know and rely on the love God has for us. God is love. Whoever lives in love lives in God, and God in them. This is how love is made complete among us so that we will have confidence on the day of judgment: In this world we are like Jesus. There is no fear in love. But perfect love drives out fear, because fear has to do with punishment. The one who fears is not made perfect in love.

We love because he first loved us. Whoever claims to love God yet hates a brother or sister is a liar. For whoever does not love their brother and sister, whom they have seen, cannot love God, whom they have not seen. And he has given us this command: Anyone who loves God must also love their brother and sister (1 Jn. 4:16–21).

Interestingly, John says that love is made complete among us and gives us confidence because, in this world, *we are like Jesus.*

There is the theme of this book in different words! It is possible to be like Jesus in this world! And walking as Jesus walked and being like him is intimately connected with love. God is love. Jesus is God. If we walk like Jesus walked and live like he lived, it is impossible not to experience and express God's love in our lives. His love fills us to overflowing with a sincere and deep love for God and others—remaining in that love maintains us in an intimate relationship with God.

Love yourself

The biblical command is *"Love your neighbor as yourself."* But you may have a problem here, at a fundamental level: you don't love yourself; in fact, you may hate yourself! Why? Because of the mistakes you have made and the damage you have done to yourself, your family, and others. Maybe your father abandoned you, or you were mocked and abused by your mother, a teacher, or someone else. Since childhood, you have believed you are bad and do not deserve to be loved. As a result, you hate yourself. That hatred can lead to self-mutilation or suicidal thoughts.

It may seem incredible, but for some people, Christ's love is the first love they have ever experienced. God's unconditional love starts to remove the self-hatred and fill your heart with love. Now you realize that God made you, and everything God does, he does well. God accepts you and receives you just as you are; you can accept yourself with all your defects. For the first time, you have hope: in Christ, you are a new creation, and God begins the process of transforming your old nature. You can accept others as they are and love them with the love you have received from God. God sets you free to love your neighbor.

Who is your neighbor? (Luke 10:25–37)

²⁵ On one occasion an expert in the law stood up to test Jesus. "Teacher," he asked, "what must I do to inherit eternal life?"

This is a well-known parable. It is impressive that the expert in the law gave the same response that Jesus did about what is most important in the law. Jesus, knowing his motive, does not answer his question—we may be too quick to explain the plan of salvation!—but asks another question:

²⁶ "What is written in the Law?" he replied. "How do you read it?"

²⁷ He answered, "'Love the Lord your God with all your heart and with all your soul and with all your strength and with all your mind'; and, 'Love your neighbor as yourself.'"

²⁸ "You have answered correctly," Jesus replied. "Do this and you will live."

We often make the Christian life very complicated. Jesus affirms here that true love for God and our neighbor is enough to gain eternal life. Of course, we know that we must trust Jesus and be born again (as we saw in John 3), but everything else flows from this foundation of love. Jesus says that if we love in this way, we will live. Do you want to live? Practice loving God and others. That's where real life is at.

²⁹ But he wanted to justify himself, so he asked Jesus, "And who is my neighbor?"

Jesus told him that he had answered correctly, but he wants more approval. It is always dangerous to try to justify ourselves before God.

³⁰ In reply Jesus said: "A man was going down from Jerusalem to Jericho, when he was attacked by robbers. They stripped him of his clothes, beat him and went away, leaving him half dead. [31] A priest happened to be going down the same road, and when he saw the man, he passed by on the other side. [32] So too, a Levite, when he came to the place and saw him, passed by on the other side. [33] But a Samaritan, as he traveled, came where the man was; and when he saw him, he took pity on him. [34] He went to him and bandaged his wounds, pouring on oil and wine. Then he put the man on his own donkey, brought him to an inn and took care of him. [35] The next day he took out two denarii and gave them to the innkeeper. 'Look after him,' he said, 'and when I return, I will reimburse you for any extra expense you may have.'

[36] "Which of these three do you think was a neighbor to the man who fell into the hands of robbers?"

[37] The expert in the law replied, "The one who had mercy on him."

Jesus told him, "Go and do likewise."

I don't think the expert in the law was expecting this explanation. Jesus loves making the hero someone looked down upon (the Samaritan), and the villain someone unexpected (the priest and Levite).

- The Samaritan was in a foreign land, where he knew the people were prejudiced against him. It would be hard for him to find lodging in Judea, and he was probably in a hurry to get home to Samaria. He lost a whole day of his journey—he would get home late, possibly to an angry and worried wife.

- He had compassion for the injured man, an important characteristic of love.

- He put the man on his own donkey.

- He tended to the man's wounds.

- He provided follow-up; he would come back to see how the man was doing and pay for his care.

How many times have you changed course and passed by on the other side when you saw someone in need? Are you willing to show the extravagant and costly love that we see in the Samaritan? Too many Christians are like the man in James 2:15–16: *Suppose a brother or a sister is without clothes and daily food. If one of you says to them, "Go in peace; keep warm and well fed," but does nothing about their physical needs, what good is it?*

Love your enemy

Loving your neighbor goes beyond helping a needy person or loving your Christian brothers and sisters. Jesus expects something radical in our relationships with others, something that goes entirely against the grain of this world. When we talk about love, it is not just for the lovable brother; Jesus demands something of us that seems almost impossible:

"You have heard that it was said, 'Love your neighbor and hate your enemy' (Matt. 5:43).

The Jews twisted and added to God's Word (as many do in the church today), like this verse from the Law:

"'Do not seek revenge or bear a grudge against anyone among your people, but love your neighbor as yourself. I am the Lord (Lev. 19:18).

The Old Testament never said to hate your enemy! Neither did it say to love your enemy, but Jesus exposes the limitations and hypocrisy of loving only the lovable—and declares that God's love (and the command to love your neighbor) includes loving your enemy:

But I tell you, love your enemies and pray for those who persecute you, that you may be children of your Father in heaven. He causes his sun to rise on the evil and the good, and sends rain on the righteous and the unrighteous. If you love those who love you, what reward will you get? Are not even the tax collectors doing that? And if you greet only your own people, what are you doing more than others? Do not even pagans do that? Be perfect, therefore, as your heavenly Father is perfect (Matt. 5:44–48).

- Loving your enemies and those who persecute you includes praying for them.

- God has an unconditional (agape) love for even the foulest sinner.

- That love is displayed in what is called "common grace," which means that many things in life are God's gifts to all humanity; Jesus mentions the sun and rain.

- Of course, we are to love our families and brothers in Christ, but even the worst sinners love those who love them. The test and proof of our love is love for an enemy.

- This is interesting to apply to daily life: Don't greet only friends and other Christians, but also people who are very different than you.

Our love is expressed in words, prayers, and deeds. It is easy to say and sing that we love God, but John says that if we do not love our neighbor, we are liars if we say we love God. Jesus knows that he is setting a high standard, but we have a high calling: To be perfect. There is no excuse for mistreating others or for a lack of love. Jesus calls us to be perfect, just as our heavenly Father is perfect. That requires incredible strength, self-control, and love.

Another summary of the Law

Jesus said that all the Law and Prophets hinge on love for God and neighbor. That focus on love makes the Christian life simple—but not easy! There is another equally impressive declaration that Jesus made, which we call "The Golden Rule:" *So in everything, do to others what you would have them do to you, for this sums up the Law and the Prophets* (Matt. 7:12). Imagine how our world would change if everyone were to put these simple commands into practice! Or the transformation in your church or family! But it starts with you. This week, try to live by the Golden Rule.

The test of our love for God (and a new commandment)

Love is a central theme of Jesus' rich teaching in the Upper Room, the night of his arrest. The command does not seem so new (the Old Testament already commanded us to love our neighbor), but this is a radical love, like Jesus' love for us.

"A new command I give you: Love one another. As I have loved you, so you must love one another. By this everyone will know that you are my disciples, if you love one another" (Jn. 13:34–35).

We don't get to choose who we love; this is Jesus' command. What does it mean to love one another? We must study Jesus' life to learn all the ways in which he loves us. It is a costly and self-sacrificial love. It is the indispensable mark of Christ's disciple, very different than what we see in the world.

The one who loves Jesus obeys him (John 14)

[21] *Whoever has my commands and keeps them is the one who loves me. The one who loves me will be loved by my Father, and I*

too will love them and show myself to them. Anyone who loves me will obey my teaching. My Father will love them, and we will come to them and make our home with them.

The simple test of our love for God is to treasure his commands and obey them, not out of obligation or fear, or trying to earn God's favor. We love him; we want to please our Savior and never grieve him.

The Father loves the person who loves his Son and obeys him. When we obey Jesus, we experience more of his love; if we don't, he still loves us! His love is unconditional, but just like an earthly father and his son, we won't enjoy the benefits of his love if we are in rebellion. We don't feel his warm embrace, and Jesus and his Father don't dwell in us. How sad! Jesus wants to reveal himself to us, but many times we miss that blessing because of our disobedience.

The one who loves lays down his life for his friends (John 15)

⁹ "As the Father has loved me, so have I loved you. Now remain in my love.¹⁰ If you keep my commands, you will remain in my love, just as I have kept my Father's commands and remain in his love. ¹¹ I have told you this so that my joy may be in you and that your joy may be complete. ¹² My command is this: Love each other as I have loved you. ¹³ Greater love has no one than this: to lay down one's life for one's friends. ¹⁷ This is my command: Love each other.

Are you still unconvinced of the importance of loving one another? How many times does Jesus have to repeat it?

Our example is the Father's love for Jesus, and Jesus' love for us. That love sent him to the cross; it is love that allows someone to give up his life for his friends.

Are you remaining in Jesus' love? If you don't feel that love, could it be that you are not obeying his commands? Is your joy complete? If not, could there be a problem with your love for God and your neighbor?

16

How to Help Others Walk with Jesus

John 4:3–42

H ave you ever shared your faith with someone? How did they respond? Many Christians are intimidated by evangelism, and most do it very rarely. But Jesus commands us to share our faith:

Therefore go and make disciples of all nations, baptizing them in the name of the Father and of the Son and of the Holy Spirit, and teaching them to obey everything I have commanded you. And surely I am with you always, to the very end of the age" (Matt. 28:19–20).

But you will receive power when the Holy Spirit comes on you; and you will be my witnesses in Jerusalem, and in all Judea and Samaria, and to the ends of the earth" (Acts 1:8).

And Jesus warned us:

"If anyone is ashamed of me and my words in this adulterous and sinful generation, the Son of Man will be ashamed of them when he comes in his Father's glory with the holy angels" (Mrk. 8:38).

If we are going to walk as Jesus walked, we have to share this amazing life with others. Here, we will walk with Jesus on his way to Galilee and learn how to connect with others and share our faith with them. Jesus was an expert in relating to people! We will also see that someone with very little knowledge of Christ can be a great evangelist.

³ So Jesus left Judea and went back once more to Galilee. ⁴ Now he had to go through Samaria.

Jesus *had* to go through Samaria?

No Jew *had* to go through Samaria. True, that was the shortest route between Judea and Galilee, but the Jews would go out of their way, following the Jordan River, to avoid Samaria. That is how much they hated the Samaritans. Why?

The Assyrians had a very effective way of controlling the many people they conquered: deport them and bring in other people to repopulate the land. When Israel was taken captive to Babylon, they brought in Assyrians, who intermarried with the remaining Jews and mixed their religions. The center of worship was a temple on Mount Gerizim, so there was no need to go to the temple in Jerusalem. When the Jews returned to the southern kingdom, instead of teaching the Samaritans the Word of God, they ridiculed them, as many Christians do with other sects that have slightly different beliefs. However, if we sincerely share with them instead of condemning them, we will find many sincere people who want to know more about Jesus. Unfortunately, it is easy for us to be like these Jews and hate people who are different than us.

Yes, Jesus had to go through Samaria, because the Father had a purpose for him there. You may need to go places no one else wants to go, because God is sending you there. He challenges our prejudices, because he loves everyone, even the Samaritans and people the world puts down. When we walk with Jesus, we will often find ourselves on a back road that no one else wants to travel.

⁵ So he came to a town in Samaria called Sychar, near the plot of ground Jacob had given to his son Joseph.⁶ Jacob's well was there, and Jesus, tired as he was from the journey, sat down by the well. It was about noon.

Did the Father tell Jesus to sit by that well? Or did he sit there because, in his human nature, he was tired and thirsty and needed a rest? It could be either, but God often uses our common sense to guide us. The well was right on time, and even though he was tired, Jesus looked for opportunities to interact with people. He knew that sooner or later someone would come to draw water; the well was a gathering place for the community.

Where is the well in your town?

It is great to pray and go to church, but if you want God to use you, you must go where the people are, open your eyes and ears, and be available to take advantage of the God-given opportunities. Where is your well? A park? Library? Mall? Health club? If you want God to use you, be sure you are not glued to your phone or a book. Be sociable!

⁷ When a Samaritan woman came to draw water, Jesus said to her, "Will you give me a drink?" ⁸ (His disciples had gone into the town to buy food.)

Provide the right atmosphere

Most likely, Jesus purposely sent the disciples to town to prepare them for future mission trips, allowing them to experience what it is like to buy lunch in a place where they obviously did not belong. But Jesus also did it to create the right conditions for personal ministry; if there had been 13 men around that well, talking and laughing, it would have been almost impossible to talk to this woman. Are there ways you can create an atmosphere conducive to meaningful conversations?

Test the waters

Jesus saw every situation as a possible divine appointment. When you walk with Jesus, God prepares the way before you. Life becomes an adventure of finding his purpose in everyone and everything that comes your way.

Don't wait for the other person to start the conversation. You may not be an extrovert; it can be hard to start talking to a stranger, but you don't have to preach or testify to them. I have seen Christians go up to a stranger and say, "The Bible says you are a sinner and you will go to hell if you don't repent and accept Christ." Unless there is an extreme Holy Spirit anointing on that person, that is the fastest way to end a conversation! Asking a small favor is a great icebreaker: "Do you have the time?" "Do you know of a good restaurant near here?" If the person responds, we press in further. If not, we wait for the next opportunity. Jesus said we would be *fishers* of men, not hunters.

It would be unusual for a woman to come to the well alone in the midday heat; it wasn't safe. Women always went together, early in the morning or late in the day. And it would be unusual for a man to talk with a woman he did not know—unless he was asking for more than water, although we will see that this woman was used to being around men. None of that stopped Jesus from initiating a conversation, but it did get the woman's attention:

⁹ The Samaritan woman said to him, "You are a Jew and I am a Samaritan woman. How can you ask me for a drink?" (For Jews do not associate with Samaritans.)

Jesus had two things against him: he was a Jew, and a man. The woman could have simply given him the water or shyly declined and left. But Jesus' request intrigued her. She did not give Jesus water—we don't know if he ever got anything to drink—but she did have a question for him. Some might take offense at what she said or feel rejected, but if you are going to be used by the Lord, you must learn to overcome offenses and manage rejection. There will be plenty of both in this world. Not everyone is as nice as you are!

How to create interest

Say or do something out of the ordinary, something radical, to surprise them. Jews saw Samaritans as unclean and would never drink from a cup offered by them. The world will notice how different you are when you love everyone and treat them with equal importance and respect. There is no place among Christians for prejudice, or any superiority based on race, class, sex, or religion.

¹⁰ Jesus answered her, "If you knew the gift of God and who it is that asks you for a drink, you would have asked him and he would have given you living water."

We tend to tell them what God's gift is, and maybe talk about something (like sin or repentance) that they cannot relate to. Instead, Jesus spoke in parables and riddles, allowing the Holy Spirit to open their understanding or permitting them to ask questions. Just as the woman ignored Jesus' request for water, Jesus ignored her question.

Go deeper

Jesus wanted to provoke interest and invite questions:

- "What is the gift of God?" God has a gift for her, but she doesn't know what it is.

- "Could God really have a gift for me? I feel like I do not deserve anything from him." Everyone loves a gift!

- "Who is this man? I have never met anyone like him!"

- "Why is he encouraging me to ask him for something? Other men have always wanted something from me!"

- "What is living water?"

This new concept of living water is directly related to their situation: they are by a well, the woman came to get water, and Jesus had just asked for a drink. Try to find a connection with the current conversation; analyze the person and look for a bridge, something they can relate to from their own experience. The idea is to offer various ways to continue the conversation and make sure they do not close up. Pay close attention to how they are responding. We are often too quick to talk about salvation and all the points of the Gospel. I have seen people looking at their watch or phone, hoping for a way to get out of being preached at.

[11] "Sir," the woman said, "you have nothing to draw with and the well is deep. Where can you get this living water? [12] Are you greater than our father Jacob, who gave us the well and drank from it himself, as did also his sons and his livestock?"

Jesus had given the woman an open door to talk about her life, but she obviously did not want to. She kept things comfortably distant and even tried to start an argument.

- Jesus spoke of living water; she could not get past the idea of natural water and how Jesus could get water without a pail. Many people do not have a clue about anything spiritual or supernatural; they are caught up in what logically makes sense to them.

- She got the idea that Jesus thought he was better than Jacob, and she defended her ancestor. People naturally resist someone who comes across as super-spiritual or arrogant.

This is a critical point. If Jesus were to engage her on her level of logic, get defensive, or argue with her, he would probably lose any chance of reaching her.

[13] *Jesus answered, "Everyone who drinks this water will be thirsty again,* [14] *but whoever drinks the water I give them will never thirst. Indeed, the water I give them will become in them a spring of water welling up to eternal life."*

One way to enter a new or closed community is to offer them something better. Thirst is a universal experience; everyone needs to drink water. Jesus does not come to us talking about spiritual things we cannot relate to; he touches us at the most basic level and offers us an abundant life. Can you think of some needs or experiences that Jesus can transform? How can you communicate that to thirsty people around you?

Living water

Jesus took advantage of her question to talk about the living water, but he recognized her hesitancy, and spoke of "everyone" and "whoever," instead of directly applying it to her. He did offer a clear option: the well water she had been used to (which never fully satisfied her thirst), and the water Jesus offered her.

Wisely, Jesus avoided religious controversies, which is almost always the best approach. And don't get defensive. Jesus effectively said he was superior to Jacob, but he offered her something better: supernatural water, which flows from his Father's heart. The water Jesus offered her (and you) is very special:

- The person who drinks living water will never thirst again. There is a fundamental difference in what Jesus offers.
- That water becomes a spring.
- It wells up inside of us.
- It has supernatural power to give us eternal life.

So why do we sing and talk about being spiritually thirsty? I suspect that many people come to church, receive a glass of living water, and feel good, but never experience the fullness of the Spirit within them and the rivers of living water that should flow from that inner fountain.

What is eternal life?

"Now this is eternal life: that they know you, the only true God, and Jesus Christ, whom you have sent" (Jn. 17:3).

Eternal life is not endless years; it is a living relationship with God. You can experience eternal life right now, in a relationship with Jesus, and you can also get a taste of it in your relationships with others. That is why Jesus' example by the well of genuinely connecting with someone is so important.

15 The woman said to him, "Sir, give me this water so that I won't get thirsty and have to keep coming here to draw water."

Like many people today, this woman was not thinking about eternal life, but only about her convenience and quality of life.

She may have been so tired of her daily life that she couldn't even think about eternal life. Many people today only want Jesus for his blessings and the promise of a better, more comfortable life. They want the blessing, not the relationship.

A common mistake

At this point, many Christians would think this woman is ready to give her life to Jesus. She did say, "Give me this water!" But there is no repentance or understanding of Jesus' lordship. It would be a superficial decision. We deceive many people when we pray with them too soon and bless them as if they are saved. Jesus did not give her the living water because he knew her heart was not right.

16 He told her, "Go, call your husband and come back."

A new approach

Instead of getting down on her for her lack of interest in spiritual things, Jesus changed his approach. I believe the Holy Spirit nudged him to talk about her marriage. When someone does not respond on a spiritual level, you can take a step of faith and go to something more personal. Listen to the Lord for some direction or revelation that may open their heart, and do not be afraid of something painful for them. Talking about family, marriage, and sex almost always gets their attention, especially, in this case, from a foreigner and a man.

17 "I have no husband," she replied.

It is here that many of us think we missed what the Spirit was saying and get discouraged. We might tend to apologize, say we need to meet our friends in town, and take off, feeling embarrassed and like a failure. However, it was there that Jesus operated in what we call a word of knowledge—a gift that God can give to any believer, which is helpful in both evangelism and within the church.

Jesus said to her, "You are right when you say you have no husband.[18] *The fact is, you have had five husbands, and the man you now have is not your husband. What you have just said is quite true."*

This whole conversation began with Jesus sitting down by a well, tired and thirsty, but God had something much more profound in mind, and now Jesus spoke with supernatural knowledge. He did not condemn her, but simply told it like it is, and that supernatural revelation confirmed to the woman that he was a man of God.

[19] *"Sir," the woman said, "I can see that you are a prophet.* [20] *Our ancestors worshiped on this mountain, but you Jews claim that the place where we must worship is in Jerusalem."*

She still won't go there! She felt uncomfortable and vulnerable discussing her personal life. The easy way out was to get into a religious argument. People do it all the time: "Who did Cain marry? His sister?" "Why does God allow so much suffering?" Or they point to all the hypocrites in the church, or the differences with Catholics, or other religious groups.

She may have really wanted to know why Jesus insisted on Jerusalem, but if we argue or condemn someone for their beliefs, we may lose them. Don't let religious arguments distract you from the real message.

True worship

[21] *"Woman," Jesus replied, "believe me, a time is coming when you will worship the Father neither on this mountain nor in Jerusalem.*

Many religious issues that seem so important to us are focused on earthly things and actually have little real relevance. Here, they provided Jesus with the opportunity to clearly present the truth. Yes, we want to respect others and avoid condemning them, but Jesus knew it was time to be upfront with her:

22 You Samaritans worship what you do not know; we worship what we do know, for salvation is from the Jews.

You need discernment to know when to confront mistaken beliefs, but if they have eternal implications, we are obligated to tell them the truth, which means we must *know* the truth to discern the error. Many want to be seen as tolerant and inclusive, yet remain quiet when presented with controversial ideas, such as the common belief that all religions lead to God. At that point, we need to speak up and say: "So what do you make of Jesus saying he is the way, the truth, and the life, and no one comes to the Father except through him? Was he lying? Or crazy? Or do you think he was telling the truth?"

23 Yet a time is coming and has now come when the true worshipers will worship the Father in the Spirit and in truth, for they are the kind of worshipers the Father seeks. 24 God is spirit, and his worshipers must worship in the Spirit and in truth."

What does it mean to worship God in Spirit and in truth? "In truth" refers to accurate knowledge of who God is and what he has done. "In Spirit" means that the place and the ways we worship really are not that important. True worship flows from our knowledge and experience, and is guided by the Holy Spirit, who always wants to exalt Jesus. Before Jesus inaugurated the new "time," temple worship consisted of rituals and laws. It was about what we do (sacrifices, offerings, reading prayers), which supposedly made us right with God. Worship was external actions, and did not necessarily have anything to do with the heart and the Spirit.

How is your worship? Do you understand what it is to worship in Spirit and truth? Do you encourage others to worship? Would you say you are one of those true worshippers whom the Father seeks?

25 The woman said, "I know that Messiah" (called Christ) "is coming. When he comes, he will explain everything to us."

Finally! The woman actually has some spiritual interest! She had some hope of a Messiah and the faith that he would explain everything to her. She may have had many questions, and getting answers was important to her, but she still kept Jesus from touching her heart.

26 Then Jesus declared, "I, the one speaking to you—I am he."

This is one of the few instances where Jesus clearly declares who he is. It gets lost in the English translation, but he uses God's name, "I AM," affirming that he indeed is God.

The Disciples return, and the woman leaves

It seems like bad timing, but we have to trust that God allowed the disciples to return just when it seemed like the woman was ready to place her faith in Jesus.

27 Just then his disciples returned and were surprised to find him talking with a woman. But no one asked, "What do you want?" or "Why are you talking with her?" 28 Then, leaving her water jar, the woman went back to the town and said to the people, 29 "Come, see a man who told me everything I ever did. Could this be the Messiah?" 30 They came out of the town and made their way toward him.

The woman probably saw the look on the disciples' faces. They were incredulous that Jesus was talking with a woman, and a Samaritan at that, although by now they were probably used to being scandalized by Jesus. She took off so fast that she left her water jar, but she became an evangelist—a better evangelist than the disciples, who had almost certainly not said a word about Jesus in that town. She was not "saved" and had minimal knowledge about Jesus, but being with Jesus changes a person, and she had faith that he could be the Messiah.

She said he "told me everything I ever did." They may have talked about much more than what is recorded in John. You do not need extensive education or experience to be an evangelist; simply invite people to come and see the Christ whom you have met.

The fields are white for the harvest

31 Meanwhile his disciples urged him, "Rabbi, eat something."

32 But he said to them, "I have food to eat that you know nothing about."

33 Then his disciples said to each other, "Could someone have brought him food?"

The woman was not the only one who was blind to spiritual things. Jesus was speaking about spiritual food, and all the disciples could think about was lunch.

34 "My food," said Jesus, "is to do the will of him who sent me and to finish his work. 35 Don't you have a saying, 'It's still four months until harvest'? I tell you, open your eyes and look at the fields! They are ripe for harvest. 36 Even now the one who reaps draws a wage and harvests a crop for eternal life, so that the sower and the reaper may be glad together. 37 Thus the saying 'One sows and another reaps' is true. 38 I sent you to reap what you have not worked for. Others have done the hard work, and you have reaped the benefits of their labor."

Jesus spoke openly with his disciples:

- They went to get food, and they were only thinking about that food. Jesus was spiritually fed by the conversation with the woman. He was sent with a purpose, and constantly sought to discern his Father's will. There was an urgency about finishing the task he was given. Do you know what your mission is? Will you know when it is finished? Have you ever felt so "full" doing the Father's work that you forgot about eating?

- They were asleep, and blinded by their sexism and racism. Many talk about a great coming harvest, but Jesus says that if you just open your eyes, there are already many people prepared for harvest.

- What is the crop God wants for us? It is people who come to know eternal life. Is your life fruitful?

- Whether sowing or reaping, evangelism should bring us joy.

- Apparently, it is unusual for the same person to sow and reap. Are you sowing the good seed of the Word, trusting that it will not return void? Are you on the lookout for people ready for the harvest?

- The disciples should be grateful for the hard work of others who faithfully preached the Word. You may be the fruit of someone who preached to your mother many years ago. Have you thought about the various people who have sown into your life?

A great Samaritan harvest

[39] *Many of the Samaritans from that town believed in him because of the woman's testimony, "He told me everything I ever did." [40] So when the Samaritans came to him, they urged him to stay with them, and he stayed two days. [41] And because of his words many more became believers.*

[42] *They said to the woman, "We no longer believe just because of what you said; now we have heard for ourselves, and we know that this man really is the Savior of the world."*

We do not know what happened with this woman. Did she marry her boyfriend? Did she continue evangelizing? Or was her part just to bring people to Jesus? We don't know, and there is no record of a church there. Interestingly, no miracle is mentioned. Elsewhere, it was the miracles that drew people to Jesus, but here it just says they believed because of his words. How wonderful! A woman with a bad reputation, who knew very little about the Bible or Jesus, was responsible for the conversion of a large part of that town. Imagine what God could do with you!

Yes, Jesus *had* to go through Samaria. God had many people there. Is there somewhere you *have* to go? Do you have your eyes open to see the fields that are ripe for harvest?

Keep on Walking

How are you doing? Have you seen any miracles or answered prayers? You may be fighting with temptation and the weakness of your flesh. But if you have put what Jesus teaches into practice, I trust that you are experiencing a closer walk with him. We have to maintain that relationship and keep walking the narrow road, but Jesus has much more for you. Get the next volume, which includes the Beatitudes, the Sermon on the Mount, and other tremendous teaching by Jesus about the Kingdom of God.

www.ingramcontent.com/pod-product-compliance
Lightning Source LLC
Chambersburg PA
CBHW060240050426

42448CB00009B/1537